This book belongs to

_____

CONTRIBUTORS

Illustrated by
Alison Atkins, Andrew Geeson, Andy Everitt Stewart,
Anglea Kincaid, Anna Cynthia Leplar, Caroline Davis,
Claire Henley, Claire Mumford, Daniel Howarth,
Dorothy Clark, Elaine Keary, Frank Endersby,
Georgia Birkett, Gillian Roberts, Jacqueline East,
Jacqueline Mair, Jan Lewis, Jane Molineaux,
Jane Swift, Jane Tattersfield, Jessica Stockham,
Jo Brown, Julie Nicholson, Karen Perrins, Kate Aldous,
Kate Davies, Linda Worrell, Liz Pichon, Louise Gardner,
Maggie Downer, Mario Capaldi, Martin Grant, Nicola Evans,
Paula Martyr, Peter Rutherford, Piers Harper, Rebecca Elgar,
Rikki O'Neill, Rory Tyger, Sara Walker, Scott Rhodes,
Serena Feneziani, Sheila Moxley, Stephanie Boey, Sue Clarke,
Terry Burton, Pauline Siewart, Lorna Bannister

Written by
Nicola Baxter, Janet Allison Brown, Andrew Charman, Jillian
Harker, Heather Henning, Alistair Hedley, Claire Keen,
Ronne Randall, Lesley Rees, Caroline Repchuk, Kay Barnes,
Gaby Goldsack, Aneurin Rhys, Louisa Somerville, Derek Hall,
Marilyn Tolhurst, Alison Morris, Nicola Edwards,
Jackie Andrews

NURSERY RHYMES

A Keepsake Treasury

Every effort has been made to acknowledge the
contributors to this book. If we have made any errors,
we will be pleased to rectify them in future editions.

This is a Parragon Publishing book
This edition published in 2003

Parragon Publishing
Queen Street House
4 Queen Street
Bath BA1 1HE, UK

Design and project management by Aztec Design

Page make-up by Caroline Reeves

ISBN 1-40542-398-6
Printed in China

NURSERY RHYMES

A Keepsake Treasury

p

Contents

CONTENTS

CONTENTS

CONTENTS

CONTENTS

CONTENTS

A Keepsake Treasury — Nursery Rhymes

Here is the Church; What's the
News of the Day; Chairs to
Mend; A Squabble 218

Epigram; Tommy Snooks and
Bessy Brooks; Three Little
Ghostesses; The Giant 219

Answers to a Child's Question 220

Dance to Your Daddy; The Cat
of Cats; Puss in the Pantry 221

The Squirrel; Tickly, Tickly;
One, Two, Three, Four, Five 222

Windy Nights; Pitter-patter 223

The Key of the Kingdom;
To Sleep Easy At Night 224

For Every Evil Under the Sun;
There Was a King and he Had
Three Daughters 225

This Little Froggy; I Am a
Gold Lock 226

The Sugar-Plum Tree; My
Mother and Your Mother 227

Mother Tabbyskins 228

Itsy Bitsy Spider; Little Boy
Blue; Ladybug! Ladybug! 230

Hickory, Dickory, Dock;
Three Blind Mice; Pop Goes
the Weasel 231

Little Robin Redbreast; Once
I Saw a Little Bird; Magpies;
Jay-bird 232

Mrs. Hen; I Had a Little Hen;
Tiggy-Touchwood 233

Matthew, Mark, Luke, and John;
How Many Miles to Babylon?;
Twinkle, Twinkle, Little Star 234

Foxy's Hole; Star Light, Star
Bright; I See the Moon 235

In Dreams; Here's a Ball for Baby;
Baby, Baby, Bunting 236

The Baby in the Cradle; Go to
Bed, Tom; Lady Moon 237

16

CONTENTS

Tucked between the rhymes there are tantalising tongue twisters bursting with alliteration.

I'm a Little Butterfly

I'm a little butterfly
   Born in a bower,
Christened in a teapot,
   Died in half an hour.

A Song

I'll sing you a song,
Nine verses long,
   For a pin;
Three and three are six,
   And three are nine;
You are a fool,
   And the pin is mine.

When the Wind...

When the wind is in the East,
   'tis neither good to man nor beast.
When the wind is in the North,
   the skilful fisher goes not forth.
When the wind is in the South,
   it blows the bait in the fish's mouth.
When the wind is in the West,
   then it is at its very best.

Little Friend

In the greenhouse lives a wren,
   Little friend of little men;
When they're good she tells them where
   To find the apple, quince, and pear.

Whole Duty of Children

A child should always say what's true,
  And speak when he is spoken to,
And behave mannerly at table:
  At least as far as he is able.

Ice Cream

Ice cream, a penny a lump!
  The more you eat,
    the more you jump.

Three Young Rats

Three young rats with black felt hats,
  Three young ducks with white straw flats,
Three young dogs with curling tails,
  Three young cats with demi-veils,
Went out to walk with two young pigs
  In satin vests and sorrel wigs;
But suddenly it chanced to rain,
  And so they all went home again.

The Camel's Complaint

Canary-birds feed on sugar and seed,
  Parrots have crackers to crunch;
And as for the poodles, they tell me the noodles
  Have chicken and cream for their lunch.
    But there's never a question
    About *my* digestion—
      Anything does for me.

Cats, you're aware, can repose in a chair,
  Chickens can roost upon rails;
Puppies are able to sleep in a stable,
  And oysters can slumber in pails.
    But no one supposes
    A poor camel dozes—
      Any place does for me.

CHARLES F. CARRYL

First

First in a carriage,
  Second in a gig,
Third on a donkey,
  And fourth on a pig.

Two Little Dogs

Two little dogs
  Sat by the fire
Over a fender of coal-dust;
Said one little dog
  To the other little dog,
If you don't talk, why, I must.

Wynken, Blynken, and Nod

Wynken, Blynken, and Nod one night
Sailed off in a wooden shoe—
Sailed on a river of crystal light,
Into a sea of dew.

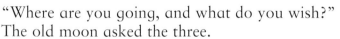

"Where are you going, and what do you wish?"
The old moon asked the three.
"We have come to fish for the herring fish
That live in this beautiful sea.

Pussycat Ate the Dumplings

Pussycat ate the dumplings,
Pussycat ate the dumplings,
Mamma stood by,
And cried, "Oh fie!
Why did you eat the dumplings?"

Cats and Dogs

Hodley, poddley, puddle, and fogs,
 Cats are to marry the poodle dogs;
Cats in blue jackets and dogs in red hats,
 What will become of the mice and the rats?

Kindness

If I had a donkey that would not go,
  Would I beat him? Oh no, no.
I'd put him in the barn and give him some corn,
  The best little donkey that ever was born.

Higgledy Piggledy

Higgledy piggledy,
  Here we lie,
Picked and plucked,
  And put in a pie!

Rain, Rain, Go Away

Rain, rain,
  Go away,
Come again
  Another day.

I Can...

I can tie my shoe lace,
  I can brush my hair,
I can wash my hands and face
  And dry myself with care.

I can clean my teeth too,
  And fasten up my frocks.
I can say, "How do you do?"
  And pull up both my socks.

To Market

To market, to market,
  To buy a plum bun;
Home again, come again,
  Market is done.

Two Little Men in a Flying Saucer

Two little men in a flying saucer
  Flew round the world one day.
They looked to the left and right a bit,
  And couldn't bear the sight of it,
And then they flew away!

Sneeze on Monday

Sneeze on Monday, sneeze for danger;
  Sneeze on Tuesday, kiss a stranger;
Sneeze on Wednesday, get a letter;
  Sneeze on Thursday, something better;
Sneeze on Friday, sneeze for sorrow;
  Sneeze on Saturday, see your
    sweetheart tomorrow.

Blow, Wind, Blow!

Blow, wind, blow! and go, mill, go!
  That the miller may grind his corn;
That the baker may take it,
  And into rolls make it,
And send us some hot in the morn.

Blow, Blow, Thou Winter Wind

Blow, blow, thou Winter wind,
Thou art not so unkind
    As man's ingratitude;
Thy tooth is not so keen,
Because thou art not seen,
    Although thy breath be rude.
Heigh ho! sing heigh ho! unto the green holly;
    Most friendship is feigning, most loving mere folly:
Then heigh ho, the holly!
    This life is most jolly.

Freeze, freeze, thou bitter sky,
Thou dost not bite so nigh
    As benefits forgot;
Though thou the waters warp,
Thy sting is not so sharp
    As friend remembered not.
Heigh ho! sing heigh ho! unto the green holly;
    Most friendship is feigning, most loving mere folly:
Then heigh ho, the holly!
    This life is most jolly.

WILLIAM SHAKESPEARE

While we were walking, we were watching window
washers wash Washington's windows with warm washing water.

A Swarm of Bees in May

A swarm of bees in May
 Is worth a load of hay;
A swarm of bees in June
 Is worth a silver spoon;
A swarm of bees in July
 Is not worth a fly.

This Little Piggy

This little piggy went to market,
 This little piggy stayed at home,
This little piggy had roast beef,
 This little piggy had none,
And this little piggy cried,
 Wee-wee-wee-wee-wee,
All the way home.

Tinker, Tailor

Tinker, tailor,
 Soldier, sailor,
Rich man, poor man,
 Beggarman, thief!

Jackanory

I'll tell you a story
Of Jackanory,
And now my story's begun;
I'll tell you another
Of Jack his brother,
And now my story's done.

Clap Your Hands

Clap your hands, clap your hands,
  Clap them just like me.
Touch your shoulders, touch your shoulders,
  Touch them just like me.
Tap your knees, tap your knees,
  Tap them just like me.
Shake your head, shake your head,
  Shake it just like me.
Clap your hands, clap your hands,
  Then let them quiet be.

Scrub Your Dirty Face

Scrub your dirty face,
  Scrub your dirty face,
With a rub-a-dub-dub,
  And a rub-a-dub-dub,
Scrub your dirty face.

Two Fat Gentlemen

Two fat gentlemen met in a lane,
    Bowed most politely, bowed once again.
How do you do? How do you do?
    How do you do again?

Two tall policemen met in a lane,
    Bowed most politely, bowed once again.
How do you do? How do you do?
    How do you do again?

Two little schoolboys met in a lane,
    Bowed most politely, bowed once again.
How do you do? How do you do?
    How do you do again?

Two thin ladies met in a lane,
    Bowed most politely, bowed once again.
How do you do? How do you do?
    How do you do again?

Baa, Baa, Black Sheep

Baa, baa, black sheep, have you any wool?
    Yes, sir, yes, sir, three bags full;
One for the master, one for the dame,
    And one for the little boy that lives down the lane.

Old Mother Goose

Old Mother Goose,
    When she wanted to wander,
Would ride through the air
    On a very fine gander.

Old Mother Hubbard

Old Mother Hubbard
    Went to the cupboard
To get her poor dog a bone;
    But when she came there
The cupboard was bare,
    And so the poor dog had none.

She went to the fishmonger's
    To buy him some fish,
And when she came back
    He was licking the dish.

She went to the hatter's
    To buy him a hat,
But when she came back
    He was feeding the cat.

There Was an Old Woman Lived under a Hill

There was an old woman
    Lived under a hill,
And if she's not gone,
    She lives there still.

There Was an Old Woman Who Lived in a Shoe

There was an old woman who lived in a shoe,
    She had so many children she didn't know
        what to do;
She gave them some broth without any bread;
    And kissed them all soundly and put them to bed.

There Was an Old Woman Went Up in a Basket

There was an old woman went up in a basket,
    Seventy times as high as the moon;
What she did there I could not but ask it,
    For in her hand she carried a broom.
"Old woman, old woman, old woman," said I,
    "Whither, oh whither, oh whither so high?"
"To sweep the cobwebs from the sky,
    And I shall be back again by and by."

Rumpty-iddity

Rumpty-iddity, row,
    row, row,
If I had a good supper,
    I could eat it now.

Anna Banana

Anna Banana
    Played the piano;
The piano broke
    And Anna choked.

Mary, Mary

Mary, Mary, quite contrary,
    How does your garden grow?
With silver bells, and cockle shells,
    And pretty maids all in a row.

Puss at the Door

Who's that ringing at my door bell?
    A little pussy cat that isn't very well.
Rub its little nose with a little mutton fat,
    That's the best cure for a little pussy cat.

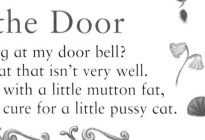

Wash, Hands, Wash

Wash, hands, wash,
    Daddy's gone to plough;
If you want your hands wash'd,
    Have them wash'd now.

A Candle

Little Nancy Etticoat
In a white petticoat,
    And a red rose.
The longer she stands
    The shorter she grows.

Address to a Child During a Boisterous Winter Evening

What way does the Wind come? What way does he go?
He rides over the water, and over the snow,
Through wood, and through vale; and o'er rocky height,
Which the goat cannot climb, takes his sounding flight;
He tosses about in every bare tree,
As, if you look up, you plainly may see;
But how he will come, and whither he goes,
There's never a scholar in England knows.

He will suddenly stop in a cunning nook,
And rings a sharp 'larum; but, if you should look,
There's nothing to see but a cushion of snow
Round as a pillow, and whiter than milk,
And softer than if it were covered with silk.

Sometimes he'll hide in the cave of a rock,
Then whistle as shrill as the buzzard cock.
Yet seek him—and what shall you find in
his place?
Nothing but silence and empty space;
Save, in a corner, a heap of dry leaves,
That he's left, for a bed, to beggars or thieves!

One Finger, One Thumb

One finger, one thumb, keep moving,
  One finger, one thumb, keep moving,
One finger, one thumb, keep moving,
  We'll all be merry and bright.

One finger, one thumb, one arm, keep moving,
  One finger, one thumb, one arm, keep moving,
One finger, one thumb, one arm, keep moving,
  We'll all be merry and bright.

One finger, one thumb, one arm, one leg, keep moving,
  One finger, one thumb, one arm, one leg, keep moving,
One finger, one thumb, one arm, one leg, keep moving,
  We'll all be merry and bright.

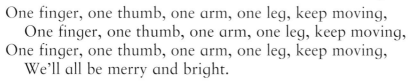

One finger, one thumb, one arm, one leg,
    one nod of the head, keep moving,
One finger, one thumb, one arm, one leg,
    one nod of the head, keep moving,
One finger, one thumb, one arm, one leg,
    one nod of the head, keep moving,
  We'll all be merry and bright.

A noisy noise annoys
an oyster.

Clap Hands

Clap hands for Daddy coming
  Down the wagon way,
With a pocketful of money
  And a cart load of hay.

Praise

Praised is he who sitteth on
  an anthill,
For he shall surely rise.

Row, Row, Row Your Boat

Row, row, row your boat,
  Gently down the stream,
Merrily, merrily, merrily, merrily,
  Life is but a dream.

The Shortest Tongue Twister

Peggy Babcock

Jack be Nimble

Jack be nimble,
      And Jack be quick:
And Jack jump over
      The candlestick.

Grig's Pig

Grandpa Grig
      Had a pig,
In a field of clover;
      Piggy died,
Grandpa cried,
      And all the fun was over.

Roses Are Red

Roses are red,
      Violets are blue,
Sugar is sweet
      And so are you.

Gift for the Queen

Pretty maid, pretty maid,
      Where have you been?
Gathering roses
      To give to the Queen.
Pretty maid, pretty maid,
      What gave she you?
She gave me a diamond,
      As big as my shoe.

One for the Mouse

One for the Mouse
One for the house,
One for the crow,
One to rot,
One to grow.

Little Poll Parrot

Little Poll Parrot
Sat in his garret
Eating toast and tea;
A little brown mouse
Jumped into the house,
And stole it all away.

Lily ladles little
Letty's lentil soup.

Three free throws.

Six thick thistle sticks.
Six thick thistles stick.

To the Snail

Snail, snail, put out your horns,
And I will give you bread
and barley corns.

This Pig

This pig got in the barn,
This ate all the corn,
This said he wasn't well,
This said he'd go and tell,
And this said—weke, weke, weke,
I can't get over the barn door sill.

There Was a Man, and his Name Was Dob

There was a man, and his name was Dob,
    And he had a wife, and her name was Mob,
And he had a dog, and he called it Cob,
    And she had a cat, called Chitterabob.
Cob, says Dob,
    Chitterabob, says Mob,
Cob was Dob's dog,
    Chitterabob Mob's cat.

Me, Myself and I

Me, myself, and I—
    We went to the kitchen and ate a pie.
Then my mother she came in
    And chased us out with a rolling pin.

Swan Swam Over the Sea

Swan swam over the sea—
    Swim, swan, swim,
Swan swam back again,
    Well swum swan.

Eeper, Weeper, Chimney Sweeper

Eeper, Weeper, Chimney sweeper,
  Married a wife and could not keep her.
Married another,
Did not love her,
  Up the chimney he did shove her!

Hey, Dorolot, Dorolot!

Hey, dorolot, dorolot!
  Hey, dorolay, dorolay!
Hey, my bonny boat, bonny boat,
  Hey, drag away, drag away!

Go to Bed

Go to bed late,
  Stay very small;
Go to bed early
  Grow very tall.

My Grandmother Sent Me

My grandmother sent me a new-fashioned three cornered cambric country cut handkerchief. Not an old-fashioned three cornered cambric country cut handkerchief, but a new-fashioned three cornered cambric country cut handkerchief.

Little Blue Ben

Little Blue Ben, who lives in the glen,
  Keeps a blue cat and one blue hen,
Which lays of blue eggs a score and ten;
  Where shall I find the little Blue Ben?

Sippity Sup

Sippity sup, sippity sup,
  Bread and milk from a china cup.
Bread and milk from a bright silver
    spoon
    Made of a piece of the bright
      silver moon.
Sippity sup, sippity sup,
  Sippity, sippity sup.

Peter Piper

Peter Piper picked a peck of pickled pepper;
  A peck of pickled pepper Peter Piper picked;
If Peter Piper picked a peck of pickled pepper,
  Where's the peck of pickled pepper Peter Piper picked?

Sunshine

A sunshiny shower
  Won't last half an hour.

Adam
and Eve
and Pinchme

Adam and Eve and Pinchme
  Went down to the river to bathe.
Adam and Eve were drowned—
  Who do you think was saved?

Old Bandy Legs

As I was going to sell my eggs,
  I met a man with bandy legs;
Bandy legs and crooked toes,
  I tripped up his heels and
    he fell on his nose.

Hannah Bantry

Hannah Bantry,
In the pantry,
  Gnawing on a mutton bone;
How she gnawed it,
How she clawed it,
  When she found herself alone.

Robert Rowley Rolled
a Round Roll Round

Robert Rowley rolled a round roll round,
  A round roll Robert Rowley rolled round;
Where rolled the round roll Robert Rowley rolled round?

Pussycat Sits by the Fire

Pussycat sits by the fire.
  How did she come there?
In walks the little dog,
  Says, "Pussy! are you there?
How do you do, Mistress Pussy?
  Mistress Pussy, how d'ye do?"
"I thank you kindly, little dog,
  I fare as well as you!"

Little Jack Horner

Little Jack Horner,
Sat in a corner,
  Eating a Christmas pie.
He put in his thumb,
And pulled out a plum,
  And said, "What a good boy am I!"

I Scream

I scream, you scream,
We all scream for ice cream!

Bow, Wow, Wow

Bow, wow, wow,
    Whose dog art thou?
"Little Tom Tinker's dog,
    Bow, wow, wow."

A Peanut

A peanut sat on the railroad track,
    His heart was all a-flutter;
Along came a train—the 9:15—
    Toot, toot, peanut butter!

Pat-a-cake, Pat-a-cake

Pat-a-cake, pat-a-cake, baker's man,
    Bake me a cake, as fast as you can.
Pat it and prick it and mark it with B,
    And put it in the oven for Baby and me.

Little Tommy Tittlemouse

Little Tommy Tittlemouse
    Lived in a little house;
He caught fishes
    In other men's ditches.

Red Stockings

Red stockings, blue stockings,
    Shoes tied up with silver;
A red rosette upon my breast
    And a gold ring on my finger.

Monday's Child is Fair of Face

Monday's child is fair of face,
    Tuesday's child is full of grace,
Wednesday's child is full of woe,
    Thursday's child has far to go,
Friday's child is loving and giving,
    Saturday's child works hard for his living,
And the child that is born on the Sabbath day
Is bonny and blithe, and good and gay.

In Lincoln Lane

I lost my mare in Lincoln Lane,
    I'll never find her there again;
She lost a shoe,
    And then lost two,
And threw her rider in the drain.

Bob Robin

Little Bob Robin,
    Where do you live?
Up in yonder wood, sir,
    On a hazel twig.

A Gentleman

If you are a gentleman,
    As I suppose you be,
You'll neither laugh nor smile
    At the tickling of your knee.

Polly Put the Kettle On

Polly put the kettle on,
　Polly put the kettle on,
Polly put the kettle on,
　We'll all have tea.

Sukey take it off again,
　Sukey take it off again,
Sukey take it off again,
　They've all gone away.

Mr. Punchinello

Oh! mother, I shall be married

　To Mr. Punchinello.
　To Mr. Punch,
　To Mr. Joe,
　To Mr. Nell,
　To Mr. Lo,
　Mr. Punch, Mr. Joe,
　Mr. Nell, Mr. Lo,
　To Mr. Punchinello.

My Small Cow

One, two, three, four,
　My small cow's legs are
　feeling poor,
Let's pull her by the tail,
　That'll cure what ails.

There Was a Little Girl

There was a little girl, and she had a little curl
   Right in the middle of her forehead;
When she was good she was very, very good,
   But when she was bad she was horrid.

Anna Maria

Anna Maria she sat on the fire;
   The fire was too hot, she sat on the pot;
The pot was too round, she sat on the ground;
   The ground was too flat, she sat on the cat;
The cat ran away with Maria on her back.

Gilly Silly Jarter

Gilly Silly Jarter,
   Who has lost a garter?
In a shower of rain,
   The miller found it,
The miller ground it,
   And the miller gave it
To Silly again.

Teeth

Thirty white horses upon a red hill,
   Now they tramp, now they champ,
Now they all stand still.

Little Jumping Joan

Here am I, little jumping Joan.
   When nobody's with me,
I'm always alone.

Goldy Locks, Goldy Locks

Goldy locks, goldy locks,
   Wilt thou be mine?
Thou shall not wash dishes,
   Nor yet feed the swine;

   But sit on a cushion,
     And sew a fine seam,
   And feed upon strawberries,
     Sugar and cream.

Hot Cross Buns!

Hot cross buns!
   Hot cross buns!
One a-penny, two a-penny,
   Hot cross buns!
If you have no daughters,
   Give them to your sons,
One a-penny, two a-penny,
   Hot cross buns!

Dingty Diddlety

Dingty diddlety,
　　My mommy's maid,
She stole oranges,
　　I am afraid;
Some in her pocket,
　　Some in her sleeve,
She stole oranges,
　　I do believe.

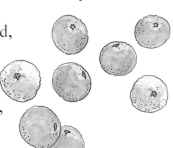

Dame Trot

Dame Trot and her cat
　　Sat down for a chat;
The dame sat on this side
　　And puss sat on that.

"Puss," says the dame,
　　"Can you catch a rat,
Or a mouse in the dark?"
　　"Purr," says the cat.

John Smith

Is John Smith within?
　　Yes, that he is.
Can he set a shoe?
　　Aye, marry, two;
Here a nail and there a nail,
　　Tick, tack, too.

Charlie Wag

Charlie Wag,
　　Charlie Wag,
Ate the pudding
　　And left the bag.

Little Hare

Round about there
　　Sat a little hare,
The bow-wows came
　　　and chased him
Right up there!

Where am I?

X, Y, and tumbledown Z,
The cat's in the cupboard
And can't see me!

Mrs. Mason

Mrs. Mason bought a basin,
    Mrs. Tyson said "What a nice one,"
"What did it cost?" asked Mrs. Frost,
    "Half a crown," said Mrs. Brown,
"Did it indeed," said Mrs. Reed,
    "It did for certain," said Mrs. Burton.
Then Mrs. Nix, up to her tricks,
    Threw the basin on the bricks.

From Wibbleton to Wobbleton

From Wibbleton to Wobbleton is fifteen miles,
    From Wobbleton to Wibbleton is fifteen miles,
From Wibbleton to Wobbleton,
    From Wobbleton to Wibbleton,
From Wibbleton to Wobbleton is fifteen miles.

Daddy

Bring Daddy home
    With a fiddle and a drum,
A pocket full of spices,
    An apple and a plum.

Little Nag

I had a little nag
    That trotted up and down;
I bridled him, and saddled him,
    And trotted out of town.

I Love Little Pussy

I love little pussy, her coat is so warm;
And if I don't hurt her she'll do me no harm.
So I'll not pull her tail nor drive her away,
But pussy and I very gently will play.

If Wishes Were Horses

If wishes were horses,
    Beggars would ride;
If turnips were watches,
    I'd wear one by my side.

Sing a Song of Sixpence

Sing a song of sixpence,
    A pocket full of rye;
Four-and-twenty blackbirds
    Baked in a pie;
When the pie was opened,
    The birds began to sing;
Wasn't that a dainty dish,
    To set before a king?

One Hen Pecking

One hen pecking in the garden—
  Mrs. MacDonald shakes her head.
Two hens pecking in the garden—
  Makes her shake her fist instead!
Three hens pecking in the garden—
  The farmer's wife comes storming out.
Four hens pecking in the garden—
  Mrs. MacDonald starts to shout.

Pease Pudding

Pease pudding hot,
  Pease pudding cold,
Pease pudding in the pot,
  Nine days old.

Some like it hot,
  Some like it cold,
Some like it in the pot,
  Nine days old.

A Pretty Little Girl in a Round-eared Cap

A pretty little girl in a round-eared cap
   I met in the streets the other day;
She gave me such a thump,
   That my heart it went bump;
I thought I should have fainted away!
   I thought I should have fainted away!

Sulky Sue

Here's Sulky Sue
   What shall we do?
Turn her face to the wall
   'Til she comes to.

We're All in the Dumps

We're all in the dumps,
For diamonds and trumps,
   The kittens are gone to St Paul's,
The babies are bit,
The moon's in a fit,
   And the houses are built without walls.

Robin the Bobbin

Robin the Bobbin,
   the big-bellied Ben,
He ate more meat than
   fourscore men;
He ate a cow, he ate a calf,
   He ate a butcher and a half;
He ate a church, he ate
   a steeple,
He ate the priest and all
   the people!
     A cow and a calf,
       An ox and a half,
     A church and a steeple,
       And all the good people,
And yet he complained that his
   stomach wasn't full.

Washing Up

When I was a little boy
   I washed my mommy's dishes;
I put my finger in one eye,
   And pulled out golden fishes.

Five Little Peas

Five little peas in a pea-pod pressed,
   One grew, two grew, and so did all the rest.
They grew, and they grew, and they did not stop,
   Until one day the pod went ... POP!

Clip, Clop

Pigs can prance,
And ducks can dance,
    Hens flutter in a flurry.
But George plods on and doesn't stop,
Clip, clop! Clip, clop!
    He's *never* in a hurry.

"Of course, I know
My horse is slow,
    But I will never worry.
For George plods on and doesn't stop,
Clip, clop! Clip, clop!
    He doesn't *need* to hurry."

Follow My Bangalorey Man

Follow my Bangalorey Man,
    Follow my Bangalorey Man;
I'll do all that ever I can
    To follow my Bangalorey Man.
We'll borrow a horse, and steal a gig,
    And round the world we'll do a jig,
And I'll do all that ever I can
    To follow my Bangalorey Man!

I Thought

I thought a thought.
But the thought I
thought wasn't the
thought I thought
I thought.

Higglety, Pigglety, Pop!

Higglety, Pigglety, pop!
    The dog has eaten the mop;
The pig's in a hurry,
    The cat's in a flurry,
Higglety, pigglety, pop!

Five Fat Sausages

Five fat sausages frying in a pan,
    All of a sudden one went "BANG!"
Four fat sausages frying in a pan, etc.
Three fat sausages frying in a pan, etc.
Two fat sausages frying in a pan, etc.
One fat sausage frying in a pan,
    All of a sudden it went "BANG!"
        and there were NO sausages left!

Pussycat Mole

Pussycat Mole,
   Jumped over a coal,
And in her best petticoat
   burnt a great hole.
Poor pussy's weeping,
   she'll have no more milk,
Until her best petticoat's
   mended with silk.

Sing, Sing

Sing, sing,
   What shall I sing?
The cat's run away
   With the pudding string!
Do, do,
   What shall I do?
The cat's run away
   With the pudding too!

I Had a Little Horse

I had a little horse,
   His name was Dappled Gray,
His head was made of gingerbread,
   His tail was made of hay.
He could amble, he could trot,
   He could carry the mustard pot,
He could amble, he could trot,
   Through the old town of Windsor.

One Little Indian

One little, two little, three little Indians
Four little, five little, six little Indians
Seven little, eight little, nine little Indians
Ten little Indian boys.

Ten little, nine little, eight little Indians
Seven little, six little, five little Indians
Four little, three little, two little Indians
One little Indian boy.

Father Short

Father Short came down the lane;
    Oh! I'm obliged to hammer and smile
From four in the morning till eight at night,
    For a bad master, and a worse dame.

Oats and Beans

Oats and beans and barley grow,
    Oats and beans and barley grow,
Do you or I or anyone know,
    How oats and beans and barley grow?

First the farmer sows his seeds,
    Then he stands and takes his ease,
Stamps his feet and claps his hands,
    Turns around to view the land.

Mr. East

Mr. East gave a feast;
    Mr. North laid the cloth;
Mr. West did his best;
    Mr. South burnt his mouth
With eating a cold potato.

Humpty Dumpty

Humpty Dumpty sat on a wall,
   Humpty Dumpty had a great fall;
All the king's horses and all the king's men
   Couldn't put Humpty together again.

A Frisky Lamb

A frisky lamb
   And a frisky child
Playing their pranks
   In a cowslip meadow:
The sky all blue
   And the air all mild
And the fields all sun
   And the lanes half-shadow.

Robin Hood

Robin Hood
   Has gone to the wood;
He'll come back again
   If we are good.

Daffy-Down-Dilly

Daffy-Down-Dilly
   Has come up to town
In a yellow petticoat
   And a green gown.

A Horse, of Course!

Who can you trust when the tractor
    breaks down,
And the nearest mechanic is off
    in the town?
Who is as big and as strong as a horse?
  Oh, silly me, a horse, of course!
Who do you know who can eat
    tons of hay,
And even munch ten sacks of oats
    in a day?
Who has an appetite large as a horse?
  Oh, silly me, a horse, of course!
Who will stick by you when you
    need a friend,
And hear all your troubles right
    through to the end?
Who is as wise and as kind as a horse?
  Oh, silly me, a horse, of course!

Cock Crow

The cock's on the wood pile
  Blowing his horn,
The bull's in the barn
  A-threshing the corn,
The maids in the meadow
  Are making the hay,
The ducks in the river
  Are swimming away.

Moo! Moo! Moo!

The Meadow Ladies Chorus,
    Is something rather new.
You'll hear them all too clearly,
    They're singing, "Moo! Moo! Moo!"

They try to trill like budgies,
    And copy blackbirds, too.
The only song they really know,
    Of course, is, "Moo! Moo! Moo!"

They practice in the morning,
    And in the night-time, too.
It doesn't make a difference though,
    They still sing, "Moo! Moo! Moo!"

Here's the Lady's Knives and Forks

Here's the lady's knives and forks.
    Here's the lady's table.
Here's the lady's looking glass.
    And here's the baby's cradle.
Rock! Rock! Rock! Rock!

Doctor Fell

I do not like thee, Doctor Fell,
    The reason why, I cannot tell;
But this I know, and know full well,
    I do not like thee, Doctor Fell.

You Need a Cow!

How does fresh milk reach your shake,
    The frothy, creamy kind you make?
You ask how?—You need a cow!

How does butter reach your bread,
    The slithery, slippery stuff you spread?
You ask how?—You need a cow!

How does your cheese reach your plate,
    The yummy, yellow kind you grate?
You ask how?—You need a cow!

How does ice cream reach your spoon,
    The kind you cannot eat too soon?
You ask how?—You need a cow!

A Face Game

Here sits the Lord Mayor; *(Forehead)*
    Here sit his two men; *(Eyes)*
Here sits the cock; *(Right cheek)*
    Here sits the hen; *(Left cheek)*
Here sit the little chickens; *(Tip of nose)*
    Here they run in, *(Mouth)*
Chinchopper, chinchopper,
    Chinchopper, chin! *(Chuck the chin)*

All Things Bright and Beautiful

All things bright and beautiful,
    All creatures great and small,
All things wise and wonderful,
    The Lord God made them all.

Each little flower that opens,
    Each little bird that sings,
He made their glowing colors,
    He made their tiny wings.

The purple-headed mountain,
    The river running by,
The sunset, and the morning,
    That brightens up the sky.

The cold wind in the winter,
    The pleasant summer sun,
The ripe fruits in the garden,
    He made them every one.

He gave us eyes to see them,
    And lips that we might tell,
How great is God Almighty,
    Who has made all things well.

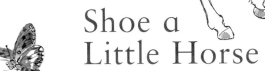

Shoe a Little Horse

Shoe a little horse,
    Shoe a little mare,
But let the little colt
    Go bare, bare, bare.

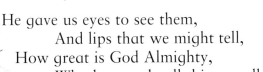

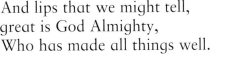

The Shepherd Boy's Song

He that is down, needs fear no fall,
    He that is low, no pride;
He that is humble, ever shall
    Have God to be his guide.

I am content with what I have,
    Little be it, or much:
And, Lord, contentment still I crave,
    Because thou savest such.

Fullness to such a burden is
    That go on pilgrimage:
Here little, and hereafter bliss
    Is best from age to age.

Buttons

Buttons, a farthing a pair,
    Come, who will buy them of me?
They are round and sound and pretty,
    And fit for the girls of the city.
Come, who will buy them of me?
    Buttons, a farthing a pair.

Turn Around

Turn around and touch the
    ground,
Turn around and touch the
    ground,
Turn around and touch the
    ground,
And fall right down.

Mary Had a Little Lamb

Mary had a little lamb,
　　Its fleece was white as snow,
And everywhere that Mary went
　　The lamb was sure to go.

It followed her to school one day,
　　Which was against the rule;
It made the children laugh and play
　　To see a lamb in school.

An Apple a Day

An apple a day
　　Sends the doctor away.
Apple in the morning
　　Doctor's warning,
Roast apple at night
　　Starves the doctor outright.

Eat an apple going to bed,
　　Knock the doctor on the head.

Three each day, seven days a week,
　　Ruddy apple, ruddy cheek.

On the Grassy Banks

On the grassy banks
　　Lambkins at their pranks;
Wooly sisters, wooly brothers,
　　Jumping off their feet,
While their wooly mothers
　　Watch them and bleat.

There Was a Piper

There was a piper, he'd a cow,
    And he'd no hay to give her;
He took his pipes and played a tune:
    "Consider, old cow, consider!"

The cow considered very well,
    For she gave the piper a penny,
That he might play the tune again,
    Of "Corn rigs are bonnie".

Rats in the Garden

Rats in the garden—catch'em Towser!
    Cows in the cornfield—run boys run!
Cat's in the cream pot—stop her now, sir!
    Fire on the mountain—run boys run!

To Market, to Market, to Buy a Fat Pig

To market, to market, to buy a fat pig,
    Home again, home again, dancing a jig;
Ride to the market to buy a fat hog,
    Home again, home again, jiggety-jog.

Cushy Cow Bonny

Cushy cow bonny, let down thy milk,
And I will give thee a gown of silk;
A gown of silk and a silver tee,
If thou wilt let down thy milk for me.

Don't-care

Don't-care didn't care;
Don't-care was wild.
Don't-care stole plum and pear
Like any beggar's child.
Don't-care was made to care,
Don't-care was hung:
Don't-care was put in the pot
And boiled till he was done.

Tweedle-dum and Tweedle-dee

Tweedle-dum and Tweedle-dee
Agreed to have a battle,
For Tweedle-dum said Tweedle-dee
Had spoiled his nice new rattle.
Just then flew down a monstrous crow,
As big as a tar-barrel,
Which frightened both the heroes so,
They quite forgot their quarrel.

Little Jack Jingle

Little Jack Jingle,
   He used to live single:
But when he got tired of this kind of life,
   He left off being single, and lived with his wife.

Young Roger Came Tapping

Young Roger came tapping at Dolly's window,
   Thumpaty, thumpaty, thump!
He asked for admittance, she answered him "No!"
   Frumpaty, frumpaty, frump!

"No, no, Roger, no! as you came you may go!"
   Stumpaty, stumpaty, stump!

Harry Parry

O rare Harry Parry,
   When will you marry?
When apples and pears are ripe.
   I'll come to your wedding,
Without any bidding,
   And dance and sing all the night.

Jack and Guy

Jack and Guy went out in the rye,
    And they found a little boy with one black eye.
Come, says Jack, let's knock him on the head.
    No, says Guy, let's buy him some bread;
You buy one loaf and I'll buy two,
    And we'll bring him up as other folk do.

The North Wind Doth Blow

The north wind doth blow,
    And we shall have snow,
And what will poor Robin do then?
    Poor thing!

He'll sit in a barn,
    And to keep himself warm,
Will hide his head under his wing.
    Poor thing!

Intery, Mintery, Cutery, Corn

Intery, mintery, cutery, corn,
    Apple seed and apple thorn.
Wire, briar, limber, lock,
    Three geese in a flock.

One flew east and one flew west;
    One flew over the cuckoo's nest.

Over the Hills and Far Away

When I was young and had no sense
   I bought a fiddle for eighteen pence,
And the only tune that I could play
   Was "Over the Hills and Far Away".

Little Fly

Little Fly,
   Thy summer's play
My thoughtless hand
   Has brushed away.

Am not I
   A fly like thee?
Or art not thou
   A man like me?

For I dance,
   And drink, and sing,
Till some blind hand
   Shall brush my wing.

Tall Shop

Tall shop in the town.
   Lifts moving up and down.
Doors swinging round about.
   People moving in and out.

If thought is life
   And strength and breath,
And the want
   Of thought is death;

Then am I
   A happy fly,
If I live
   Or if I die.

WILLIAM BLAKE

Bat, Bat

Bat, Bat, come under my hat,
And I'll give you a slice of bacon,
And when I bake I'll give you a cake,
If I am not mistaken.

Jello on the Plate

Jello on the plate,
Jello on the plate,
Wibble, wobble,
Wibble, wobble,
Jello on the plate.

Candies in the jar,
Candies in the jar,
Shake them up,
Shake them up,
Candies in the jar.

Candles on the cake,
Candles on the cake,
Blow them out,
Blow them out,
Puff, PUFF, PUFF!

Two Little Dicky Birds

Two little dicky birds sitting on a wall,
One named Peter, one named Paul.
Fly away, Peter!
Fly away, Paul!
Come back, Peter!
Come back, Paul!

I Had a Little Cow

I had a little cow;
   Hey-diddle, ho-diddle!
I had a little cow, and it had a little calf;
   Hey-diddle, ho-diddle; and there's my song half.

I had a little cow;
   Hey-diddle, ho-diddle!
I had a little cow, and I drove it to the stall;
   Hey-diddle, ho-diddle; and there's my song all!

The Cherry Tree

Once I found a cherry stone,
   I put it in the ground,
And when I came to look at it,
   A tiny shoot I found.

The shoot grew up and up each day,
   And soon became a tree.
I picked the rosy cherries then,
   And ate them for my tea.

Rub-a-dub Dub

Rub-a-dub dub,
   Three men in a tub,
And who do you think they be?
   The butcher, the baker,
The candle-stick maker,
   Turn them out knaves all three.

Aiken Drum

There was a man lived in the moon,
  and his name was Aiken Drum
And he played upon a ladle,
  and his name was Aiken Drum.

And his hat was made of good cream cheese,
  and his name was Aiken Drum.

And his coat was made of good roast beef,
  and his name was Aiken Drum.

And his buttons were made of penny loaves,
  and his name was Aiken Drum.

His waistcoat was made of crust of pies,
  and his name was Aiken Drum.

His breeches were made of haggis bags,
  and his name was Aiken Drum.
And he played upon a ladle,
  and his name was Aiken Drum.

ANONYMOUS
SCOTTISH

Lavender's Blue

Lavender's blue, dilly, dilly, lavender's green,
  When I am king, dilly, dilly, you shall be queen;
Call up your men, dilly, dilly, set them to work,
  Some to the plough, dilly, dilly, some to the cart;
Some to make hay, dilly, dilly, some to thresh corn;
  Whilst you and I, dilly, dilly, keep ourselves warm.

The Eagle

He clasps the crag with crooked hands;
  Close to the sun in lonely lands,
Ring'd with the azure world, he stands.
The wrinkled sea beneath him crawls;
  He watches from his mountain walls,
And like a thunderbolt he falls.

ALFRED, LORD TENNYSON

Ten Green Bottles

Ten green bottles, standing on a wall,
   Ten green bottles, standing on a wall,
And if one green bottle should accidentally fall,
   There'd be nine green bottles, standing on a wall.

Nine green bottles, standing on a wall,
   Nine green bottles, standing on a wall,
And if one green bottle should accidentally fall,
   There'd be eight green bottles, standing on a wall.

Eight green bottles, standing on a wall,
   Eight green bottles, standing on a wall,
And if one green bottle should accidentally fall,
   There'd be seven green bottles, standing on a wall.

(continue with seven green bottles, then six green
bottles etc...)

A big black
bug bit a
big black
bear, made
the big
black bear
bleed blood.

The Cold Old House

I know a house, and a cold old house,
   A cold old house by the sea.
If I were a mouse in that cold old house
   What a cold, cold mouse I'd be!

Three Wise Old Women

Three wise old women were they, were they,
    Who went to walk on a winter day:
One carried a basket to hold some berries,
    One carried a ladder to climb for cherries,
The third, and she was the wisest one,
    Carried a fan to keep off the sun.

But they went so far, and they went so fast,
    They quite forgot their way at last,
So one of the wise women cried in a fright,
    "Suppose we should meet a bear tonight!
Suppose he should eat me!"
    "And me!!" "And me!!!"
"What is to be done?" cried all the three.

Whether they ever sailed home again,
    Whether they saw any bears, or no,
You must find out, for I don't know.

I Bought an Old Man

Hey diddle diddle,
    And hey diddle dan!
And with a little money,
    I bought an old man.
His legs were all crooked
    And wrong ways set on,
So what do you think
    Of my little old man?

Birds of a Feather

Birds of a feather flock together
    And so will pigs and swine;
Rats and mice shall have their choice,
    And so shall I have mine.

Duck's Ditty

All along the backwater,
    Through the rushes tall,
Ducks are a-dabbling.
    Up tails all!

Ducks' tails, drakes' tails,
    Yellow feet a-quiver,
Yellow bills all out of sight
    Busy in the river!

Slushy green undergrowth
    Where the roach swim—
Here we keep our larder,
    Cool and full and dim.

Every one for what he likes!
    We like to be
Heads down, tails up,
    Dabbling free!

High in the blue above
    Swifts whirl and call—
We are down a-dabbling
    Up tails all!

There Was
an Old Crow

There was an old crow
    Sat upon a clod:
There's an end of my song,
    That's odd!

The Kangaroo

Old Jumpety-Bumpety-Hop-and-Go-One
    Was lying asleep on his side in the sun.
This old kangaroo, he was whisking the flies
    (With his long glossy tail)
        from his ears and his eyes.
Jumpety-Bumpety-Hop-and-Go-One
    Was lying asleep on his side in the sun,
Jumpety-Bumpety-Hop!

Jack, Jack

Jack, Jack, the bread's a-burning,
    All to a cinder;
If you don't come and fetch it out
    We'll throw it through the window.

Tom, Tom, the Piper's Son

Tom, Tom, the piper's son,
    Stole a pig, and away he run.
The pig was eat, and Tom was beat,
    And Tom went roaring down the street.

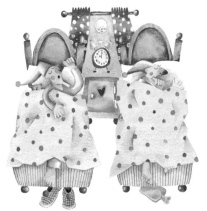

Robin and Richard

Robin and Richard were two young men;
    They laid in bed till the clock struck ten;
Then up starts Robin and looks at the sky,
    Oh! brother Richard, the sun's very high:

The bull's in the barn threshing the corn,
    The cock's on the dunghill blowing his horn,
The cat's at the fire frying of fish,
    The dog's in the pantry breaking his dish.

I Had a Little Nut Tree

I had a little nut tree, nothing would it bear,
But a silver nutmeg, and a golden pear;
The King of Spain's daughter came to visit me,
And all for the sake of my little nut tree.
I skipped over water, I danced over sea,
And all the birds of the air couldn't catch me.

To Daffodils

Fair daffodils, we weep to see
You haste away so soon;
As yet the early-rising Sun
Has not attain'd his noon.
Stay, stay
Until the hasting day
Has run
But to the even song;
And, having pray'd together, we
Will go with you along.

The Apple Tree

Here is the tree with leaves so green.
Here are the apples that hang between.
When the wind blows the apples fall.
Here is a basket to gather them all.

Egg Hatching Dream

When Jenny is sitting,
  And sitting, and sitting,
She can't take up knitting,
  Or sew a fine seam.

If her eggs are to hatch,
  Every one of the batch,
There is nothing to match,
  An egg-hatching dream.

Her thoughts travel far and near.
  Half-asleep she'll appear,
Until she starts to hear,
  Her eggs start to crack!

Billy Billy Booster

Billy Billy Booster,
  Had a little rooster,
The rooster died
  And Billy cried.
Poor Billy Booster.

The Wise Old Owl

There was an old owl who lived in an oak;
  The more he heard, the less he spoke.
The less he spoke, the more he heard.
  Why aren't we like that wise old bird!

Here We Go Round the Mulberry Bush

Here we go round the mulberry bush,
   The mulberry bush, the mulberry bush,
Here we go round the mulberry bush,
   On a cold and frosty morning.

This is the way we wash our hands,
   Wash our hands, wash our hands,
This is the way we wash our hands,
   On a cold and frosty morning.

Here we go round the mulberry bush,
   The mulberry bush, the mulberry bush,
Here we go round the mulberry bush,
   On a cold and frosty morning.

This is the way we wash our clothes,
   Wash our clothes, wash our clothes,
This is the way we wash our clothes,
   On a cold and frosty morning.

Here we go round the mulberry bush,
   The mulberry bush, the mulberry bush,
Here we go round the mulberry bush,
   On a cold and frosty morning.

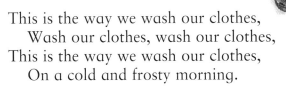

Dancing Round the Maypole

Dancing round the maypole,
  Dancing all the day,
Dancing round the maypole,
  On the first of May,
Dancing round the maypole,
  What a merry bunch,
Dancing round the maypole,
  Till it's time for lunch.

Dancing round the maypole,
  Shouting out with glee,
Dancing round the maypole,
  Till it's time for tea.
Dancing round the maypole,
  Blue and white and red,
Dancing round the maypole,
  Till it's time for bed.

The Ostrich

Here is the ostrich straight and tall,
  Nodding his head above us all.
Here is the hedgehog prickly and small,
  Rolling himself into a ball.
Here is the spider scuttling around,
  Treading so lightly on the ground.
Here are the birds that fly so high,
  Spreading their wings across the sky.
Here are the children fast asleep,
  And in the night the owls do peep,
"Tuit tuwhoo, tuit tuwhoo!"

Wooly Coats

In the middle of the winter,
  All the animals complain,
"Our furry coats are much too thin.
  They let the icy north wind in.
We want to go indoors again!"
But while the rest all shiver,
  Sheep are fine and look quite smug,
"We will not come to any harm.
  We are the warmest on the farm.
Our wooly coats will keep us snug!"

Where Are You?

Doris Duck, Doris Duck,
  Where are you?
Here I am! Here I am!
  Dabbling in the dew.
Dora Duck, Dora Duck,
  Where are you?
Here I am, diving down,
  Which I love to do!
Ducklings all, ducklings all,
  Where are you?
Here we are, swimming round,
  Coming to splash YOU!

Counting Sheep

Old MacDonald's counting sheep,
    But not because he cannot sleep.
You see, he's wondering if maybe,
    Each sheep has now had her baby.
"Stand still!" he cries. "Be still and steady,
    I might have counted you already!"

Poor Old MacDonald's feeling dizzy!
    Then suddenly he starts to smile.
"Goodbye! I'll see you in a while."

When all the farm is soundly sleeping,
    Old MacDonald's softly creeping.
It's really easy to count sheep,
    When you're awake and they're asleep!

Michael Finnegan

There was an old man called Michael Finnegan
    He grew whiskers on his chinnegan
The wind came out and blew them in again
    Poor old Michael Finnegan. Begin again...

Loves to Sing

Old MacDonald loves to sing,
  Whilst doing all his chores.
His wife just thanks her lucky stars,
  He does it when outdoors!

It's rather like a lost lamb's bleat,
  A hungry horse's neigh.
The kind of snort a piglet makes,
  When rolling in the hay!

So Old MacDonald's wife just cooks,
  Her husband gets no thinner,
Because MacDonald cannot sing,
  With his mouth full of dinner!

Kittens
Are Cuddly

Kittens are cuddly,
  Kittens are sweet,
They dash round the farmyard,
  On soft, furry feet.

And before very long,
  They are kittens no more,
But cats who do nothing,
  But stretch out and snore!

Busy Farmer

When a very busy farmer,
   Goes upstairs to bed at night,
He simply can't stop wondering,
   If everything's all right.

Are the cows asleep and dreaming?
   Are they trotting down the lane?
Is the rooster in the kitchen,
   Pecking at the pies again?

So a very busy farmer,
   Always rises at first light.
He simply cannot wait to check
   That everything's all right.

I am a Pretty Little Dutch Girl

I am a pretty little Dutch girl,
   As pretty as I can be.
And all the boys in the
     neighborhood
   Are crazy over me!

Without a Growl

When Old MacDonald's work is done,
And twilight falls with the setting sun,
   He sits down in his chair.
For he knows that he has a friend,
From day's beginning to day's end,
   Bruce the farm dog is there.

The Great Brown Owl

The brown owl sits in the ivy bush,
  And she looketh wondrous wise,
With a horny beak beneath her cowl,
  And a pair of large round eyes.

She sat all day on the selfsame spray,
  From sunrise till sunset;
And the dim, gray light it was all too bright
  For the owl to see in yet.

"Jenny Owlet, Jenny Owlet," said a merry little bird,
  "They say you're wondrous wise;
But I don't think you see, though you're looking at me
  With your large, round, shining eyes."

But night came soon, and the pale white moon
  Rolled high up in the skies;
And the great brown owl flew away in her cowl,
  With her large, round, shining eyes.

As Small As a Mouse

As small as a mouse,   As tall as a house,
  As wide as a bridge,   As straight as a pin.

Tommy Thumb

Tommy Thumb, Tommy Thumb,
    Where are you?
Here I am, here I am,
    How do you do?

Peter Pointer, Peter Pointer,
    Where are you?
Here I am, here I am,
    How do you do?

Middle Man, Middle Man,
    Where are you?
Here I am, here I am,
    How do you do?

Ruby Ring, Ruby Ring,
    Where are you?
Here I am, here I am,
    How do you do?

Baby Small, Baby Small,
    Where are you?
Here I am, here I am,
    How do you do?

Fingers all, fingers all,
    Where are you?
Here we are, here we are,
    How do you do?

Solomon Grundy

Solomon Grundy,
    Born on Monday,
Christened on Tuesday,
    Married on Wednesday,
Sick on Thursday,
    Worse on Friday,
Died on Saturday,
    Buried on Sunday,
That was the end
    Of Solomon Grundy.

Old Joe Brown

Old Joe Brown, he had a wife,
 She was all of eight feet tall.
She slept with her head in the kitchen,
 And her feet stuck out in the hall.

The Little Bird

This little bird flaps its wings,
 Flaps its wings,
  flaps its wings,
This little bird flaps its wings,
 And flies away
  in the morning!

Old John Muddlecombe

Old John Muddlecombe lost his cap,
 He couldn't find it anywhere, the poor old chap.
He walked down the High Street, and everybody said,
 "Silly John Muddlecombe, you've got it on your head!"

Poor Old Robinson Crusoe!

Poor old Robinson Crusoe!
   Poor old Robinson Crusoe!
They made him a coat
   Of an old nanny goat,
I wonder how they could do so!
   With a ring a ting tang,
   And a ring a ting tang,
Poor old Robinson Crusoe!

Jack Sprat

Jack Sprat could eat no fat,
   His wife could eat no lean,
And so between the two of them
   They licked the platter clean.

Cock-a-doodle-doo!

Cock-a-doodle-doo!
   My dame has lost her shoe,
My master's lost his fiddling stick,
   And doesn't know what to do.

Cock-a-doodle-doo!
   What is my dame to do?
Till master finds his fiddling stick,
   She'll dance without her shoe.

Cock-a-doodle-doo!
   My dame has found her shoe,
And master's found his fiddling stick,
   Sing cock-a-doodle-doo!

The Lion and the Unicorn

The lion and the unicorn
    Were fighting for the crown:
The lion beat the unicorn
    All round the town.
Some gave them white bread,
    Some gave them brown:
Some gave them plum-cake
    And drummed them out of town.

Hark, Hark

Hark, hark,
    The dogs do bark,
Beggars are coming to town:
    Some in rags,
    Some in tags,
And some in velvet gowns.

Did you Know?

Did you know ducks like to dance?
    Their pirouettes are grand.
And what is more,
    They can perform
On water or on land.

Did you know ducks like to dance?
    They shimmy and they shake.
And what is more,
    They can perform
A very fine Swan Lake!

There Was a Little Turtle

There was a little turtle,
    He lived in a box.
He swam in a puddle,
    He climbed on the rocks.

He snapped at a mosquito,
    He snapped at a flea.
He snapped at a minnow,
    He snapped at me.

He caught the mosquito,
    He caught the flea.
He caught the minnow,
    But... he didn't catch me!

Watch Out

When Percy the pig feels peckish,
    There's very little doubt,
That he will gobble anything,
    Animals, watch out!
He nibbles straw
    At the stable door.
He chomps on weed
    Where the ducklings feed.
He munches hay
    When the cows are away.
He snacks on corn
    If a sack is torn.
When Percy the pig feels peckish,
    There's very little doubt,
That even Old MacDonald
    Shouldn't leave his lunch about!

Slowly, Slowly

Slowly, slowly, very slowly
  Creeps the garden snail.

Slowly, slowly, very slowly
  Up the garden rail.

Quickly, quickly, very quickly
  Runs the little mouse.

Quickly, quickly, very quickly
  Round about the house.

The Owl

When cats run home and light is come,
  And dew is cold upon the ground,
And the far-off stream is dumb,
  And the whirring sail goes round,
  And the whirring sail goes round;
Alone and warming his five wits,
  The white owl in the belfry sits.

For Want of a Nail

For want of a nail, the shoe was lost;
  For want of the shoe, the horse was lost;
For want of the horse, the rider was lost;
  For want of the rider, the battle was lost;
For want of the battle, the kingdom was lost;
  And all for the want of a horseshoe nail.

Little Trotty Wagtail

Little Trotty Wagtail, he went in the rain,
    And twittering, tottering sideways, he ne'er got straight again;
He stooped to get a worm, and looked up to get a fly,
    And then he flew away 'ere his feathers they were dry.

Little Trotty Wagtail, he waddled in the mud,
    And left his little foot-marks, trample where he would,
He waddled in the water-pudge, and waggle went his tail,
    And chirrupped up his wings to dry upon the garden rail.

Little Trotty Wagtail, you nimble all about,
    And in the dimpling water-pudge you waddle in and out;
        Your home is nigh at hand and in the warm pig-stye;
        So, little Master Wagtail, I'll bid you a good-bye.

JOHN CLARE

A Farmyard Song

I had a cat and the cat pleased me,
    I fed my cat by yonder tree;
Cat goes fiddle-i-fee.

I had a hen and the hen pleased me,
    I fed my hen by yonder tree;
Hen goes chimmy-chuck, chimmy-chuck,
    Cat goes fiddle-i-fee.

I had a duck and the duck pleased me,
    I fed my duck by yonder tree;
Duck goes quack, quack,
    Hen goes chimmy-chuck, chimmy-chuck,
Cat goes fiddle-i-fee.

Gee up, Neddy

Gee up, Neddy,
    Don't you stop,
Just let your feet go
    Clippety clop.
Clippety clopping,
    Round and round.
Giddy up,
    We're homeward bound.

Old Macdonald

Old Macdonald had a farm,
   E...I...E...I...O
And on that farm he had
   some cows,
   E...I...E...I...O
With a moo-moo here,
   And a moo-moo there,
Here a moo, there a moo,
   Everywhere a moo-moo,
Old Macdonald had a farm,
   E...I...E...I...O.

Old Macdonald had a farm,
   E...I...E...I...O
And on that farm he had
   some ducks,
   E...I...E...I...O
With a quack-quack here,
   And a quack-quack there,
Here a quack, there a quack,
   Everywhere a quack-quack,
Old Macdonald had a farm,
   E...I...E...I...O.

One Misty Moisty Morning

One misty moisty morning,
   When cloudy was the weather,
There I met an old man
   Clothed all in leather;

Clothed all in leather,
   With cap under his chin—
How do you do, and how do you do,
   And how do you do again!

This is the Way the Ladies Ride

This is the way the ladies ride:
    Tri, tre, tre, tree,
    Tri, tre, tre, tree!
This is the way the ladies ride:
    Tri, tre, tre, tri-tre-tre-tree!

This is the way the gentlemen ride:
    Gallop-a-trot,
    Gallop-a-trot!
This is the way the gentlemen ride:
    Gallop-a-gallop-a-trot!

This is the way the farmers ride:
    Hobbledy-hoy,
    Hobbledy-hoy!
This is the way the farmers ride:
    Hobbledy hobbledy-hoy!

This is the way the butcher boy rides,
    Tripperty-trot,
    Tripperty-trot.
Till he falls in a ditch
    With a flipperty,
    Flipperty, flop, flop, FLOP!

Marching

March, march, head erect,
    Left, right, that's correct.

Three Little Kittens

Three little kittens they lost their mittens,
  And they began to cry,
Oh, mother dear, we sadly fear
  That we have lost our mittens.

What! lost your mittens, you naughty kittens!
  Then you shall have no pie.
Mee-ow, mee-ow, mee-ow.
  No, you shall have no pie.

The three little kittens they found their mittens,
  And they began to cry,
Oh, mother dear, see here, see here,
  For we have found our mittens.

Put on your mittens, you silly kittens,
  And you shall have some pie.
Purr-r, purr-r, purr-r,
  Oh, let us have some pie.

Catch Him, Crow!

Catch him, crow!
  Carry him, kite
Take him away till the
  apples are ripe;
When they are ripe and
  ready to fall,
Here comes a baby,
  apples and all.

Goosey, Goosey, Gander

Goosey, goosey, gander,
    Whither shall I wander?
Upstairs and downstairs,
    And in my lady's chamber.
There I met an old man
    Who would not say his prayers.
I took him by the left leg
    And threw him down the stairs.

Wine and Cakes

Wine and cakes for gentlemen,
    Hay and corn for horses,
A cup of ale for good old wives,
    And kisses for the lasses.

Jack and Jill

Jack and Jill went up the hill
    To fetch a pail of water;
Jack fell down and broke his crown
    And Jill came tumbling after.

Up Jack got and home did trot
    As fast as he could caper;
He went to bed to mend his head
    With vinegar and brown paper.

Back on the Farm

Old MacDonald went to town,
 Three pigs under his arm.
One didn't want to go there,
 So he ran back to the farm.

Old MacDonald went to town,
 Two pigs under his arm.
One kicked the farmer on his knee,
 And ran back to the farm.

Old MacDonald went to town,
 One pig under his arm.
He bit the farmer on the nose,
 Then ran back to the farm.

The piglets didn't want to go,
 They said, "We like it here!"
MacDonald said, "Oh, all right then!"
 And the pigs began to cheer!

One-One was a racehorse.
 Two-Two was one, too.
When One-One won one race,
 Two-Two won one, too.

Diddlety, Diddlety

Diddlety, diddlety, dumpty,
The cat ran up the plum tree;
Half a crown to fetch her down,
Diddlety, diddlety, dumpty.

Girls and Boys, Come Out to Play

Girls and boys, come out to play;
   The moon doth shine as bright as day;
Leave your supper, and leave your sleep,
   And come with your playfellows into the street.

Come with a whoop, come with a call,
   Come with a good will or not at all.
Up the ladder and down the wall,
   A halfpenny roll will serve us all.
You find milk, and I'll find flour,
   And we'll have a pudding in half-an-hour.

There Was...

There was a girl
   in our town,
Silk an' satin was
   her gown,
Silk an' satin, gold
   an' velvet.
Guess her name, three
   times I've telled it.

Sure the ship's
shipshape, sir.

Knick, Knack, Paddy Whack

This old man, he played one,
   He played knick knack on my drum.
With a knick knack paddy whack, give a dog a bone,
   This old man went rolling home.

This old man, he played two,
   He played knick knack on my shoe.
With a knick knack paddy whack, give a dog a bone,
   This old man went rolling home.

A Tudor

A Tudor who tooted a flute, tried to tutor two tooters to toot. Said the two to their tutor, "Is it harder to toot or to tutor two tooters to toot?"

A Cat Came Fiddling

A cat came fiddling out of a barn,
   With a pair of bagpipes under her arm;
She could sing nothing but fiddle cum fee,
   The mouse has married the humble-bee.
Pipe, cat—dance, mouse,
   We'll have a wedding at our good house.

Oh Dear, What Can the Matter Be?

Oh dear, what can the matter be?
   Dear, dear, what can the matter be?
Oh dear, what can the matter be?
   Johnny's so long at the fair.

He promised he'd buy me a basket of posies,
   A garland of lilies, a garland of roses,
A little straw hat to set off the blue ribbons
   That tie up my bonny brown hair.

Oh dear, what can the matter be?
   Dear, dear, what can the matter be?
Oh dear, what can the matter be?
   Johnny's so long at the fair.

Greedy Tom

Jimmy the Mowdy
   Made a great crowdy;
Barney O'Neal
   Found all the meal;
Old Jack Rutter
   Sent two stone of butter;
The Laird of the Hot
   Boiled it in his pot;
And Big Tom of the Hall
   He supped it all.

A Rat

There was a rat,
   for want of stairs,
Went down a rope
   to say his prayers.

Richard Dick

Richard Dick upon a stick,
    Sampson on a sow,
We'll ride away to Colley fair
    To buy a horse to plough.

Milking

Cushy cow, bonny, let down thy milk,
    And I will give thee a gown of silk;
A gown of silk and a silver tee,
    If thou wilt let down thy milk for me.

Bow-wow

Bow-wow, says the dog,
    Mew, mew, says the cat,
Grunt, grunt, goes the hog,
    And squeak goes the rat.
Tu-whu, says the owl,
    Caw, caw, says the crow,
Quack, quack, says the
        duck,
    And what cuckoos say
        you know.

Punctuality

Be always in time,
    Too late is a crime.

Jeremiah

Jeremiah
   Jumped in the fire.
Fire was so hot
   He jumped in the pot.
Pot was so little
   He jumped in the kettle.
Kettle was so black
   He jumped in the crack.
Crack was so high
   He jumped in the sky.
Sky was so blue
   He jumped in a canoe.
Canoe was so deep
   He jumped in the creek.
Creek was so shallow
   He jumped in the tallow.
Tallow was so soft
   He jumped in the loft.

Mrs. White

Mrs. White had a fright
   In the middle of the night.
She saw a ghost, eating toast,
   Halfway up a lamp post.

Cows graze in groves
on grass which grows
in grooves in groves.

Parliament Soldiers

High diddle ding, did you hear the bells ring?
   The parliament soldiers are gone to the king.
Some they did laugh, and some they did cry,
   To see the parliament soldiers go by.

The Robin and the Wren

The robin and the wren,
    They fought upon the porridge pan;
But before the robin got a spoon,
    The wren had eaten the porridge down.

Ride Away, Ride Away

Ride away, ride away,
    Johnny shall ride,
He shall have a pussycat
    Tied to one side;
He shall have a little dog
    Tied to the other,
And Johnny shall ride
    To see his grandmother.

Betty and Bob brought
back blue balloons
from the big
bazaar.

Willie Wastle

I, Willie Wastle,
    Stand on my castle,
An' a' the dogs o' your toon,
    Will no' drive Willie Wastle down.

The Old Woman's Three Cows

There was an old woman had three cows,
    Rosy and Colin and Dun.
Rosy and Colin were sold at the fair,
    And Dun broke her heart in a fit of despair,
So there was an end of her three cows,
    Rosy and Colin and Dun.

The Mischievous Raven

A farmer went trotting upon his gray mare,
    Bumpety, bumpety, bump!
With his daughter behind him so rosy and fair,
    Lumpety, lumpety, lump!

A raven cried, "Croak!" and they all tumbled down,
    Bumpety, bumpety, bump!
The mare broke her knees and the farmer his crown,
    Lumpety, lumpety, lump!

The mischievous raven flew laughing away,
    Bumpety, bumpety, bump!
And vowed he would serve them the same next day,
    Lumpety, lumpety, lump!

Pit, Pat

Pit, pat, well-a-day,
Little Robin flew
        away;
Where can little
    robin be?
Gone into the
    cherry tree.

Mother?

"Mother, may I go out to swim?"
    "Yes, my darling daughter.
Fold your clothes up neat and trim,
    But don't go near the water."

A Tree Toad Loved a She-toad

A tree toad loved a she-toad
  Who lived up in a tree.
He was a two-toed tree toad
  But a three-toed toad was she.

The two-toed tree toad tried to win
  The three-toed she-toad's heart,
For the two-toed tree toad loved
    the ground
  That the three-toed tree toad trod.

But the two-toed tree toad tried in vain.
  He couldn't please her whim.
From her tree toad bower with her
    three-toed power
  The she-toad vetoed him.

My Hamster

My hamster tears up paper
  'Cos that's what hamsters do.
He isn't being naughty
  But hamsters like to chew!

My brother's homework's missing.
  It's in my hamster's cage.
My hamster is quite happy.
  My brother's in a rage!

My hamster just chews paper
  To make himself a nest,
So why are they all shouting,
  "That hamster is a pest!"

Susan Shineth Shoes and Socks

Susan shineth shoes and socks;
  Socks and shoes shines Susan.
She ceased shining shoes and socks,
  For shoes and socks shock Susan.

Bless You

Bless you, bless you, burnie-bee,
  Tell me when my wedding be;
If it be tomorrow day,
  Take your wings and fly away.
Fly to the east, fly to the west,
  Fly to him I love the best.

A Bear for Everyone

There are tall bears and small bears,
  Bears of every size;
Bears in jerkins, bears in sweaters,
  Bears in smart bow ties.

There are bears with fur that's long,
  Bears with fur that's short;
Fur that's curly, fur that's straight
  And fur of every sort.

There are bears in every brown shade
  That you have ever seen;
There are bears in rainbow colors,
  Yellow, red and green.

One thing that makes teddy bears
  Such enormous fun,
Is if you look hard, you will find
  A bear for everyone.

Fred's Ted

If there has been some trouble,
  It's no use blaming Fred.
It's never Fred who's done it.
  It's always his old Ted.

It's Ted who gets up early,
  And wakes up Mom and Dad,
And then seems to be surprised
  When both of them get mad.

It's old Ted who quite often
  Leaves Fred's room in a mess;
And though he says he's tidied,
  You'd never really guess.

She Sells Sea Shells

She sells sea shells
by the sea shore.
The shells she sells
are surely seashells.
So if she sells shells
on the seashore,
I'm sure she sells
seashore shells.

It's Ted who's put his paw prints
  On newly painted walls,
Then claims that he has never
  Been near the walls at all.

It's Fred who really tries hard
  To make old Ted be good,
But old Ted never, ever does
  What good teddies should!

Spin, Dame

Spin, Dame, spin,
  Your bread you must win;
Twist the thread and break it not,
  Spin, Dame, spin.

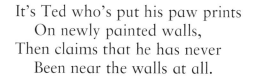

Hark the Robbers

Hark at the robbers going through,
  Through, through, through;
    through, through, through;
Hark at the robbers going through,
  My fair lady.

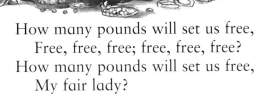

What have the robbers done to you,
  You, you, you; you, you, you?
What have the robbers done to you,
  My fair lady?

How many pounds will set us free,
  Free, free, free; free, free, free?
How many pounds will set us free,
  My fair lady?

Stole my gold watch and chain,
  Chain, chain, chain; chain,
    chain, chain;
Stole my gold watch and chain,
  My fair lady.

A hundred pounds will set you free,
  Free, free, free; free, free, free;
A hundred pounds will set you free,
  My fair lady.

Jack Sprat

Jack Sprat had a cat,
  It had but one ear;
It went to buy butter
  When butter was dear.

There Was a Crooked Man

There was a crooked man,
   and he went a crooked mile,
He found a crooked sixpence
   against a crooked stile;
He bought a crooked cat, which
   caught a crooked mouse,
And they all lived together in
   a little crooked house.

The Flying Pig

Dickery, dickery, dare,
   The pig flew up in the air;
The man in brown
   Soon brought him down,
Dickery, dickery, dare.

Three Wise Men of Gotham

Three wise men of Gotham
   Went to sea in a bowl:
And if the bowl had been stronger,
   My song would have been longer.

I Saw a Slippery, Slithery Snake

I saw a slippery, slithery snake
   Slide through the grasses,
Making them shake.
   He looked at me with his beady eye.
"Go away from my pretty green garden," said I.
   "Sssss," said the slippery, slithery snake,
As he slid through the grasses,
   Making them shake.

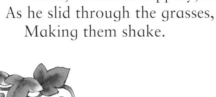

Tommy's Shop

Tommy kept a chandler's shop,
   Richard went to buy a mop;
Tommy gave him such a whop,
   That sent him out of the
chandler's shop.

Shoes

Baby's shoes,

Mother's shoes,

Father's shoes,

Policeman's shoes,

GIANT'S SHOES!

Head, Shoulders, Knees and Toes

Head, shoulders, knees and toes, knees and toes,
   Head, shoulders, knees and toes, knees and toes,
And eyes and ears and mouth and nose,
   Head, shoulders, knees and toes, knees and toes.

The Little Turtle Dove

High in the pine tree,
  The little turtle dove
Made a little nursery
  To please her little love.

"Coo," said the turtle dove,
  "Coo," said she;
In the long, shady branches
  Of the dark pine tree.

Rain, Rain

Rain, rain,
  go to Spain,
Never show
  your face again.

Green Cheese

Green cheese,
Yellow laces,
Up and down
The market places.

As I was going to St. Ives

As I was going to St. Ives,
  I met a man with seven wives.
Each wife had seven sacks,
  Each sack had seven cats,
Each cat had seven kits.
  Kits, cats, sacks, and wives,
  How many were going to St Ives?

Five Little Soldiers

Five little soldiers
    Standing in a row,
Three stood straight,
    And two stood—so.
Along came the captain,
    And what do you think?
They ALL stood straight,
    As quick as a wink.

Betty Botter

Betty Botter bought some butter,
    "But," she said, "this butter's bitter
If I put it in my batter,
    It will make my batter bitter.
But a bit of better butter,
    That would make my batter better."
So she bought a bit of butter,
    Better than her bitter butter,
And she put it in her batter,
    And the batter was not bitter.
So 'twas better Betty Botter
    Bought a bit of better butter.

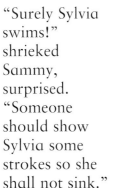

"Surely Sylvia
swims!"
shrieked
Sammy,
surprised.
"Someone
should show
Sylvia some
strokes so she
shall not sink."

Peter Works With One Hammer

Peter works with one hammer, one hammer, one hammer,
Peter works with one hammer, this fine day.

Peter works with two hammers, two hammers, two hammers,
Peter works with two hammers, this fine day.

Peter's very tired now, tired now, tired now,
Peter's very tired now, this fine day.

Peter's going to sleep now, sleep now, sleep now,
Peter's going to sleep now, this fine day.

Peter's waking up now, up now, up now,
Peter's waking up now, this fine day.

A skunk sat on a stump
and thunk the stump
stunk, but the stump
thunk the skunk stunk.

With My Hands on Myself

With my hands on myself, what have we here?
  This is my brainbox, nothing to fear.
Brainbox and wibbly wobbly woos,
  That's what they taught me when I went to school.

With my hands on myself, what have we here?
  These are my eye-peepers, nothing to fear.
Eye-peepers, brainbox and wibbly wobbly woos,
  That's what they taught me when I went to school.

Clap, Clap Hands

Clap, clap hands, one, two, three,
  Put your hands upon your knees,
Lift them up high to touch the sky,
  Clap, clap hands and
    away they fly.

Hey, My Kitten

Hey, my kitten, my kitten,
  And hey my kitten, my deary,
Such a sweet pet as this
  There is not far not neary.
Here we go up, up, up,
  Here we go down, down, downy;
Here we go backwards and fowards,
  And here we go round, round,
    roundy.

You Can Take a Bear Anywhere

Did you know that
   you can take a bear
Absolutely anywhere?

On a bus, or in a train;
To the beach in the sun;
   For a walk in the rain.

In a bag with you to school;
Or wrapped in a towel
   To the swimming pool.

In a pocket of your coat,
To the park to help you
   To sail your boat.

Best of all, to bed at night,
Under the blankets,
   Snuggled up tight.

I always take my
   teddy bear,
Absolutely anywhere.

My Little Maid

Hey diddle doubt,
   My candle's out,
My little maid's not at home;
   Saddle the hog,
   And bridle the dog,
And fetch my little maid home.

Home she came, trittity trot,
   She asked for the porridge she left in the pot;
Some she ate, and some she shod,
   And some she gave to the truckler's dog.

I Met a Man

As I was going up
   the stair
I met a man who
   wasn't there.
He wasn't there
   again today—
Oh! how I wish
   he'd go away!

Ickle, Ockle

Ickle, ockle, blue bockle,
Fishes in the sea,
If you want a pretty maid,
Please choose me.

Jim Crow

Twist about, turn about,
Jump Jim Crow;
Every time I wheel about
I do just so.

Acrobatic Bear

I am an acrobatic bear.
I can stand on my head.
I somersault and touch my toes,
By bouncing on the bed.

I can do a row of cartwheels,
Along the garden wall,
And balance on the clothes line,
With no trouble at all.

I can swing, hanging upside down,
From the old climbing frame,
And score at least a dozen goals,
In any soccer game.

It's true I have a willing friend,
Who gives a helping hand,
But these things are tricky for a bear,
As I'm sure you'll understand.

The Three Jovial Welshmen

There were three jovial Welshmen,
　　As I have heard them say,
And they would go a-hunting
　　Upon St David's day.

All the day they hunted,
　　And nothing could they find
But a ship a-sailing,
　　A-sailing with the wind.

One said it was a ship;
　　The other he said nay;
The third said it was a house,
　　With the chimney blown away.

And all the night they hunted,
　　And nothing could they find
But the moon a-gliding,
　　A-gliding with the wind.

Robinets and Jenny Wrens

Robinets and Jenny Wrens
　　Are God Almighty's
　　　　cocks and hens.

The martins and the swallows
　　Are God Almighty's bows
　　　　and arrows.

Six slippery
snails slid
slowly
seaward.

Five Little Monkeys

Five little monkeys walked along the shore;
   One went a-sailing,
Then there were four.

Four little monkeys climbed up a tree;
   One of them tumbled down,
Then there were three.

Three little monkeys found a pot of glue;
   One got stuck in it,
Then there were two.

   Two little monkeys found a currant bun;
      One ran away with it,
         Then there was one.

      One little monkey cried all afternoon,
         So they put him in an airplane
            And sent him to the moon.

Four Stiff Standers

Four stiff standers,
   Four dilly-danders,
Two lookers,
   Two crookers,
And a wig-wag!

Lovely lemon
liniment.

I Love Sixpence

I love sixpence, pretty little sixpence,
  I love sixpence better than my life;
I spent a penny of it, I spent another,
  And took fourpence home to my wife.

Oh, my little fourpence, pretty little fourpence,
  I love fourpence better than my life;
I spent a penny of it, I spent another,
  And I took twopence home to my wife.

Oh, my little twopence, my pretty little twopence,
  I love twopence better than my life;
I spent a penny of it, I spent another,
  And I took nothing home to my wife.

I saw Esau kissing
Kate. I saw Esau,
he saw me, and
she saw I saw Esau.

Oh, my little nothing, my pretty little nothing,
  What will nothing buy for my wife?
I have nothing, I spend nothing,
  I love nothing better than my wife.

The soldiers
shouldered
shooters on
their shoulders.

Cross Patch

Cross patch,
  Draw the latch,
Sit by the fire and spin;
  Take a cup,
  And drink it up,
Then call your neighbors in.

One, Two, Buckle my Shoe

One, two,
   Buckle my shoe;
Three, four,
   Shut the door;
Five, six,
   Pick up sticks;
Seven, eight,
   Lay them straight;
Nine, ten,
   A good fat hen;

Eleven, twelve,
   Who will delve?
Thirteen, fourteen,
   Maids a-courting;
Fifteen, sixteen,
   Maids a-kissing;
Seventeen, eighteen,
   Maid a-waiting;
Nineteen, twenty,
   My stomach's empty.

Doctor Foster Went to Gloucester

Doctor Foster went to Gloucester,
   In a shower of rain;
He stepped in a puddle, up to
     his middle,
   And never went there again.

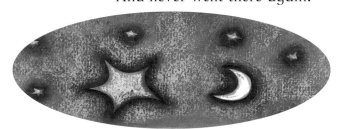

A Star

I have a little sister, they call her Peep, Peep;
   She wades the waters deep, deep, deep;
She climbs the mountains high, high, high;
   Poor little creature she has but one eye.

I Went up One Pair of Stairs

I went up one pair of stairs.
  Just like me.
I went up two pairs of stairs.
  Just like me.
I went into a room.
  Just like me.
    I looked out of a window.
      Just like me.
        And there I saw a monkey.
          Just like me.

Ten Little Fingers

I have ten little fingers,
  And they all belong to me.
I can make them do things,
  Would you like to see?

I can shut them up tight,
  Or open them all wide.
Put them all together,
  Or make them all hide.

I can make them jump high;
  I can make them jump low.
I can fold them quietly,
  And hold them all just so.

A Thorn

I went to the wood and got it;
  I sat me down and looked at it;
The more I looked at it the less I liked it;
  And I brought it home because I couldn't help it.

This is the House That Jack Built

This is the house that Jack built.

This is the malt
   That lay in the house that Jack built.

This is the rat,
   That ate the malt
That lay in the house that Jack built.

This is the cat,
   That killed the rat,
That ate the malt
   That lay in the house that Jack built.

This is the dog,
   That worried the cat,
That killed the rat,
   That ate the malt,
That lay in the house that
Jack built.

My Hands

My hands upon my head I place,
   On my shoulders, on my face;
On my hips I place them so,
   Then bend down to touch my toe.

Now I raise them up so high,
   Make my fingers fairly fly,
Now I clap them, one, two, three.
   Then I fold them silently.

You Can Cuddle a Kitten

You can cuddle a kitten,
 And stroke a dog.
But it's hard to cuddle up
  to a frog.

A budgie can talk to you,
 Tell you its name.
A chat with a bat just isn't
  the same.

A stick
  insect is easy,
 It stays in one place.
But spiders surprise you
   by tickling your face.

If you're choosing an animal,
 Make sure that you get
Something that's certain to make
 a good pet!

I Am the Music Man

I am the music man,
I come from far away,
 And I can play.
What can you play?
 I play piano.
Pia, pia, piano, piano, piano,
Pia, pia, piano, pia, piano.

I am the music man,
I come from far away,
 And I can play.
What can you play?
 I play the big drum.
Boomdi, boomdi, boomdi boom,
 Boomdi boom, boomdi boom,
Boomdi, boomdi, boomdi boom,
 Boomdi, boomdi, boom.
Pia, pia, piano, piano, piano,
Pia, pia, piano, pia, piano.

Please Tell Me Why...

"Come on, tortoise!" says my mom,
    When I'm too slow getting dressed.
Can't she see that I don't wear a shell
    And that all I have on is my vest?

Dad calls me a mischievous monkey,
    But I don't see how that can be.
I don't have a tail, I'm not
      covered in fur,
    Though I'm quite good at
    climbing, you see.

Mom calls me "night owl",
      when I can't sleep,
    Though I don't hoot and I don't
    have wings.
And I certainly do not have feathers,
    And owls must have all of those
    things.

It's true that I slither into their bed.
    'Cos I like to say "Hi!" when I wake.
But my skin isn't scaly, so please tell me why
    Dad says, "Here comes that wriggly snake"?

These Are Grandma's Glasses

These are Grandma's glasses,
    This is Grandma's hat;
Grandma claps her hands like this,
    And rests them in her lap.

These are Grandpa's glasses,
    This is Grandpa's hat;
Grandpa folds his arms like this,
    And has a little nap.

I'm a Little Teapot

I'm a little teapot short and stout,
    Here's my handle, here's my spout,
When I get my steam up hear me shout,
    Tip me up and pour me out.

Pettitoes

The pettitoes are little feet,
    And the little feet not big;
Great feet belong to the grunting hog,
    And the pettitoes to the little pig.

Okey Cokey

You put your left arm in, your left arm out,
   In, out, in, out, you shake it all about,
You do the okey cokey, and you turn around,
   And that's what it's all about.

Oh, the okey cokey,
   Oh, the okey cokey,
Oh, the okey cokey,
   Knees bend, arms stretch,
Ra, ra, ra!

Mousie

Mousie comes a-creeping,
   creeping.
Mousie comes a-peeping,
   peeping.
Mousie says, "I'd like to
   stay,
But I haven't time today."
Mousie pops into his
   hole
And says, "ACHOO!
   I've caught a cold!"

Build a House With Five Bricks

Build a house with five bricks,
   One, two, three, four, five.
Put a roof on top,
   And a chimney too,
Where the wind blows through!

Johnny Morgan

Little Johnny Morgan,
    Gentleman of Wales,
Came riding on a nanny-goat,
    Selling of pigs' tails.

Five Little Ducks

Five little ducks went swimming one day,
    Over the hills and far away,
Mother Duck said, "Quack, quack, quack, quack,"
    But only four little ducks came back.
One little duck went swimming one day,
    Over the hills and far away,
Mother Duck said, "Quack, quack, quack, quack,"
    And all the five little ducks came back.

Can you imagine
an imaginary
menagerie
manager imagining
managing an
imaginary menagerie?

Diddle, Diddle, Dumpling

Diddle, diddle, dumpling, my son John
    Went to bed with his trousers on;
One shoe off, the other shoe on,
    Diddle, diddle, dumpling, my son John.

When Famed King Arthur Ruled This Land

When famed King Arthur ruled this land
   He was a goodly king:
He took three pecks of barley meal
   To make a bag pudding.

A rare pudding the king did make,
   And stuffed it well with plums;
And in it put such lumps of fat,
   As big as my two thumbs.

The king and queen did eat thereof,
   And noblemen beside,
And what they could not eat that night
   The queen next morning fried.

Twelve twins twirled twelve twigs.

Fat frogs flying past fast.

Many an anemone sees an enemy anemone.

The blue bluebird blinks.

Six short slow shepherds.

What is the Rhyme for Porringer?

What is the rhyme for *porringer*?
   The King he had a daughter fair,
And gave the Prince of Orange her.

The Story of Flying Robert

When the rain comes tumbling down
  In the country or the town.
All good little girls and boys
  Stay at home and mind their toys.
Robert thought, "No, when it pours,
  It is better out of doors."
Rain it *did*, and in a minute
  Bob was in it.
Here you see him, silly fellow,
  Underneath his red umbrella.

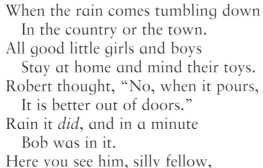

What a wind! Oh! how it whistles
    Through the trees and flowers and thistles!
It has caught his red umbrella;
    Now look at him, silly fellow,
Up he flies to the skies.
    No one heard his screams and cries,
Through the clouds the rude wind bore him,
    And his hat flew on before him.

Soon they got to such a height,
    They were nearly out of sight!
And the hat went up so high
    That it really touched the sky.
No one ever yet could tell
    Where they stopped or where they fell:
Only, this one thing is plain,
    Bob was never seen again!

DR HEINRICH HOFFMANN

Little Wind

Little wind, blow on the hill-top;
    Little wind, blow down the plain;
Little wind, blow up the sunshine;
        Little wind, blow off the rain.

KATE GREENAWAY

A Child's Laughter

All the bells of heaven may ring,
  All the birds of heaven may sing,
All the wells on earth may spring,
  All the winds on earth may bring
  All sweet sounds together;
Sweeter far than all things heard,
  Hand of harper, tone of bird,
Sound of woods at sundown stirred,
  Welling water's winsome word,
Wind in warm wan weather.

Golden bells of welcome rolled
  Never forth such notes, nor told
Hours so blithe in tones so bold,
  As the radiant mouth of gold
  Here that rings forth heaven.
If the golden-crested wren
  Were a nightingale—why, then,
Something seen and heard of men
  Might be half as sweet as when
Laughs a child of seven.

ALGERNON CHARLES SWINBURNE

Ozymandias

I met a traveler from an antique land
    Who said: Two vast and trunkless legs of stone
Stand in the desert... Near them, on the sand,
    Half sunk, a shattered visage lies, whose frown,
And wrinkled lip, and sneer of cold command,
    Tell that its sculptor well those passions read
Which yet survive, stamped on these lifeless things,
    The hand that mocked them, and the heart that fed:
And on the pedestal these words appear:
    "My name is Ozymandias, king of kings:
Look on my works, ye Mighty, and despair!"
    Nothing beside remains. Round the decay
Of that colossal wreck, boundless and bare
    The lone and level sands stretch far away.

PERCY BYSSHE SHELLEY

When That I Was and a Little Tiny Boy

When that I was and a little tiny boy,
　　With hey, ho, the wind and the rain;
A foolish thing was but a toy,
　　For the rain it raineth every day.

But when I came to man's estate,
　　With hey, ho, the wind and the rain;
'Gainst knaves and thieves men shut their gate,
　　For the rain it raineth every day.

A great while ago the world begun,
　　With hey, ho, the wind and the rain;
But that's all one, our play is done,
　　And we'll strive to please you every day.

WILLIAM SHAKESPEARE

Jemmy Dawson

Brave news is come to town,
　　Brave news is carried;
Brave news is come to town,
　　Jemmy Dawson's married.

First he got a porridge-pot,
　　Then he bought a ladle;
Then he got a wife and child,
　　And then he bought a cradle.

I Remember, I Remember

I remember, I remember
    The house where I was born,
The little window where the sun
    Came peeping in at morn;
He never came a wink too soon
    Nor brought too long a day;
But now, I often wish the night
    Had borne my breath away.

I remember, I remember
    The fir trees dark and high;
I used to think their slender tops
    Were close against the sky:
It was a childish ignorance,
    But now 'tis little joy
To know I'm farther off from Heaven
    Than when I was a boy.

THOMAS HOOD

The Dumb Soldier

When the grass was closely mown,
    Walking on the lawn alone,
In the turf a hole I found
    And hid a soldier underground.

Spring and daisies came apace;
    Grasses hid my hiding-place;
Grasses run like a green sea
    O'er the lawn up to my knee.

Under grass alone he lies,
    Looking up with leaden eyes,
Scarlet coat and pointed gun,
    To the stars and to the sun.

When the grass is ripe like grain,
    When the scythe is stoned again,
When the lawn is shaven clear,
    Then my hole shall reappear.

I shall find him, never fear,
    I shall find my grenadier;
But, for all that's gone and come,
    I shall find my soldier dumb.

ROBERT LOUIS STEVENSON

Meet on the Road

"Now, pray, where are you going?" said Meet-on-the Road.
  "To school, sir, to school sir," said Child-as-it-Stood.
"What have you in your basket, child?" said Meet-on-the-Road.
  "My dinner, sir, my dinner, sir," said Child-as-it-Stood.

"What have you for dinner, child?" said Meet-on-the-Road.
  "Some pudding, sir, some pudding, sir," said Child-as-it-Stood.
"Oh, then I pray, give me a share," said Meet-on-the-Road.
  "I've little enough for myself, sir," said Child-as-it-Stood.

"Pray, what are those bells ringing for?" said Meet-on-the Road.
  "To ring bad spirits home again," said Child-as-it Stood.
"Oh, then I must be going, child!" said Meet-on-the-Road.
  "So fare you well, so fare you well," said Child-as-it-Stood.

ANONYMOUS
SCOTTISH

Where Go the Boats?

Dark brown is the river,
  Golden is the sand.
It flows along for ever,
  With trees on either hand.

Green leaves a-floating,
  Castles of the foam,
Boats of mine a-boating—
  Where will all come home?

On goes the river,
  And out past the mill,
Away down the valley,
  Away down the hill.

Away down the river,
  A hundred miles or more,
Other little children
  Shall bring my boats ashore.

ROBERT LOUIS STEVENSON

Eldorado

Gaily bedight
  A gallant knight,
In sunshine and in shadow,
  Had journeyed long,
  Singing a song,
In search of Eldorado.

But he grew old—
  This knight so bold—
And o'er his heart a shadow
  Fell as he found
  No spot of ground
That looked like Eldorado.

And, as his strength
  Failed him at length,
He met a pilgrim shadow:
  "Shadow," said he,
  "Where can it be,
This land of Eldorado?"

"Over the mountains
  Of the Moon,
Down the valley of the shadow,
  "Ride, boldly ride,"
  The shade replied,
"If you seek for Eldorado."

EDGAR ALLAN POE

The Oxen

Christmas Eve, and twelve of the clock.
   "Now they are all on their knees,"
An elder said as we sat in a flock
   By the embers in hearthside ease.

We pictured the meek mild creatures,
Where they dwelt in their strawy pen,
Nor did it occur to one of us there
   To doubt they were kneeling then.

So fair a fancy few would weave
   In these years! Yet, I feel,
If someone said on Christmas Eve,
   "Come; see the oxen kneel

"In the lonely barton by yonder coomb

Christmas Eve

On Christmas Eve I turned
   the spit,
I burnt my fingers, I feel it
   yet;
The little cock sparrow flew
   over the table,
The pot began to play with
   the ladle.

Our childhood used to know,"
I should go with him in the gloom,
Hoping it might be so.

THOMAS HARDY

Christmas Bells

I heard the bells on Christmas Day
    Their old familiar carols play,
And wild and sweet
    The words repeat
Of Peace on earth, Good-will to men!

And thought how, as the day had
        come,
    The belfries of all Christendom
Had rolled along
    The unbroken song
Of Peace on earth, Good-will to men!

Then from each black accursed mouth,
    The cannon thundered in the South,
And with the sound
    The carols drowned,
The Peace on earth, Good-will to men!

And in despair I bowed my head;
    "There is no peace on earth,"
        I said,
"For hate is strong
    And mocks the song
Of Peace on earth, Good-will to men!"

Then peeled the bells more loud
        and deep:
    "God is not dead, nor doth
        he sleep!
The Wrong shall fail,
    The Right prevail,
With Peace on earth,
    Good-will to men!"

HENRY WADSWORTH LONGFELLOW

Georgie, Porgie, Pudding, and Pie

Georgie, Porgie, pudding, and pie,
    Kissed the girls and made them cry;
When the boys came out to play
    Georgie Porgie ran away.

See a Pin and Pick it Up

See a pin and pick it up,
    All the day you'll have good luck;
See a pin and let it lay,
    Bad luck you'll have all the day!

The Duel

The gingham dog and the calico cat
   Side by side on the table sat;
'Twas half-past twelve, and
     (what do you think!)
   Nor one nor t'other had slept a wink!
The old Dutch clock and the Chinese plate
   Appeared to know as sure as fate
There was going to be a terrible spat.
   (I wasn't there; I simply state
   What was told to me by the Chinese plate!)

The gingham dog went "Bow-wow-wow!"
   And the calico cat replied "mee-ow!"
The air was littered, an hour or so,
   With bits of gingham and calico,
While the old Dutch clock in the
     chimney-place
   Up with its hands before its face,
For it always dreaded a family row!
   (Now mind: I'm only telling you
   What the old Dutch clock declares is true!)

EUGENE FIELD

Mr. Nobody

Mr. Nobody is a nice young man,
He comes to the door with his hat in his hand.
Down she comes, all dressed in silk,
A rose in her bosom, as white as milk.
She takes off her gloves, she shows me her ring,
Tomorrow, tomorrow, the wedding begins.

Three Children Sliding on the Ice

Three children sliding on the ice
Upon a summer's day,
As it fell out, they all fell in,
The rest they ran away.

Now had these children been at home,
Or sliding on dry ground,
Ten thousand pounds to one penny
They had not all been drowned.

You parents all that children have,
And you that have got none,
If you would have them safe abroad,
Pray keep them safe at home.

Little Sally Waters

Little Sally Waters,
   Sitting in the sun,
Crying and weeping,
   For a young man.
Rise, Sally, rise,
   Dry your weeping eyes,
Fly to the east,
   Fly to the west,
Fly to the one you love the best.

The Grand Old Duke of York

The grand old Duke of York,
   He had ten thousand men;
He marched them up to the top of the hill,
   And he marched them down again!

And when they were up they were up,
   And when they were down they were down;
And when they were only halfway up,
   They were neither up nor down.

To a Butterfly

I've watched you now a full half-hour,
    Self-poised upon that yellow flower;
And, little Butterfly! indeed
    I know not if you sleep or feed.
How motionless!—not frozen seas
    More motionless! And then
What joy awaits you, when the breeze
    Hath found you out among the trees,
And calls you forth again!

This plot of orchard-ground is ours;
    My trees they are, my Sister's flowers.
Here rest your wings when they are weary;
    Here lodge as in a sanctuary!
Come often to us, fear no wrong;
    Sit near us on the bough!
We'll talk of sunshine and of song,
    And summer days, when we were young;
Sweet childish days, that were as long
    As twenty days are now.

WILLIAM WORDSWORTH

Ring-a-ring o'roses

Ring-a-ring o'roses,
    A pocket full of posies,
A-tishoo! A-tishoo!
    We all fall down!

Caterpillar

Brown and furry
    Caterpillar in a hurry,
Take your walk
    To the shady leaf, or stalk,
Or what not,
    Which may be the
        chosen spot.
No toad spy you,
    Hovering bird of prey
        pass by you;
Spin and die,
    To live again a butterfly.

CHRISTINA ROSSETTI

My Little Cow

I had a little cow,
    Hey diddle, ho diddle!
I had a little cow,
    and I drove it to the stall;
hey diddle, ho diddle!
    and there's my song all.

The Snake

A narrow fellow in the grass
   Occasionally rides;
You may have met him,—did you not?
   His notice sudden is.

The grass divides as with a comb,
   A spotted shaft is seen;
And then it closes at your feet
   And opens further on.

He likes a boggy acre,
   A floor too cool for corn.
Yet when a child, and barefoot,
   I more than once, at morn,

Have passed, I thought, a whip-lash
   Unbraiding in the sun,—
When, stooping to secure it,
   It wrinkled, and was gone.

EMILY DICKINSON

Way Down Yonder in the Maple Swamp

Way down yonder in the maple swamp
   The wild geese gather and the ganders honk;
The mares kick up and the ponies prance;
   The old sow whistles and the little pigs dance.

The Cow

The friendly cow all red and white,
   I love with all my heart:
She gives me cream with all her might,
   To eat with apple-tart.

She wanders lowing here and there,
   And yet she cannot stray,
All in the pleasant open air,
   The pleasant light of day.

And blown by all the winds that pass
   And wet with all the showers,
She walks among the meadow grass
   And eats the meadow flowers.

Gray Goose and Gander

Gray goose and gander,
   Waft your wings together,
And carry the good king's daughter
   Over the one strand river.

Calico Pie

Calico Pie,
   The little Birds fly
Down to the calico tree,
   Their wings were blue,
And they sang "Tilly-loo!"
   Till away they flew,—
And they never came back to me!
   They never came back!
They never came back!
   They never came back to me!

Calico Jam,
   The little Fish swam,
Over the syllabub sea,
   He took off his hat,
To the Sole and the Sprat,
   And the Willeby-wat,—
But he never came back to me!
   He never came back!
He never came back!
   He never came back to me!

EDWARD LEAR

The Robins

A robin and a robin's son
   Once went to town to buy a bun.
They couldn't decide on a plum or plain,
   And so they went back home again.

I Eat My
Peas With Honey

I eat my peas with honey,
   I've done it all my life,
   It makes the peas
      taste funny,
      But it keeps
         them on
            my knife.

The Fairies

Up the airy mountain,
    Down the rushy glen,
We daren't go a-hunting
    For fear of little men;
Wee folk, good folk,
    Trooping all together;
Green jacket, red cap,
    And white owl's feather!

Down along the rocky shore
    Some make their home;
They live on crispy pancakes
    Of yellow tide-foam;
Some in the reeds
    Of the black mountain lake,
With frogs for their watch-dogs,
    All night awake.

Little Husband

I had a little husband,
    No bigger than my thumb;
I put him in a pint pot
    And there I bade him drum.
I gave him some garters
    To garter up his hose,
And a little silk handkerchief
    To wipe his pretty nose.

The Merchants of London

Hey diddle dinkety, poppety, pet,
    The merchants of London they
        wear scarlet;
Silk in the collar and gold in the hem,
    So merrily march the merchant men.

The Fieldmouse

Where the acorn tumbles down,
　　There the ash tree sheds its berry,
With your fur so soft and brown,
　　With your eye so round and merry,
Scarcely moving the long grass,
　　Fieldmouse, I can see you pass.

Little thing, in what dark den,
　　Lie you all the winter sleeping?
Till warm weather comes again,
　　Then once more I see you peeping
Round about the tall tree roots,
　　Nibbling at their fallen fruits.

Fieldmouse, fieldmouse, do not go,
　　Where the farmer stacks his treasure,
Find the nut that falls below,
　　Eat the acorn at your pleasure,
But you must not steal the grain
　　He has stacked with so much pain.

Make your hole where mosses spring,
　　Underneath the tall oak's shadow,
Pretty, quiet, harmless thing,
　　Play about the sunny meadow.
Keep away from corn and house,
　　None will harm you, little mouse.

CECIL FRANCES ALEXANDER

Tyger! Tyger!

Tyger! Tyger! burning bright
   In the forests of the night,
What immortal hand or eye
   Could frame thy fearful symmetry?

In what distant deeps or skies
   Burnt the fire of thine eyes?
On what wings dare he aspire?
   What the hand dare seize the fire?

And what shoulder, and what art,
   Could twist the sinews of thy heart?
And, when thy heart began to beat,
   What dread hand? and what dread feet?

What the hammer? what the chain?
   In what furnace was thy brain?
What the anvil, what dread grasp
   Dare its deadly terrors clasp?

When the stars threw down their spears,
   And water'd heaven with their tears,
Did he smile his work to see?
   Did he who made the Lamb make thee?

Tyger! Tyger! burning bright
   In the forests of the night,
What immortal hand or eye,
   Dare frame thy fearful symmetry?

WILLIAM BLAKE

The Wedding

Pussicat, wussicat, with a white foot,
  When is your wedding and I'll come to it.
The beer's to brew, and the bread's to bake,
  Pussicat, wussicat, don't be too late.

Fishes Swim

Fishes swim in water clear,
  Birds fly up into the air,
Serpents creep along the ground,
  Boys and girls run round and round.

Oliver Twist

Oliver Twist
  You can't do this,
So what's the use
  Of trying?
Touch your toe,
  Touch your knee,
Clap your hands,
  Away we go.

You Shall be Queen

Lilies are white,
  Rosemary's green,
When I am king,
  You shall be queen.

Little Robin and Pussycat

Little Robin Redbreast jumped upon a wall,
    Pussycat jumped after him, and almost got a fall!
Little Robin chirped and sang, and what did pussy say?
    Pussy cat said, "Mew" and Robin jumped away.

Little Robin Redbreast sat upon a tree,
    Up went pussycat, and down went he!
Down came pussy, and away Robin ran;
    Says little Robin Redbreast, "Catch me if you can!"

The Mouse's Lullaby

Oh, rock-a-by, baby mouse, rock-a-by, so!
    When baby's asleep to the baker's I'll go,
And while he's not looking I'll pop from a hole,
    And bring to my baby a fresh penny roll.

Cut Thistles

Jerry Hall

Jerry Hall,
    He is so small,
A rat could eat him,
    Hat and all.

Cut thistles in May,
    They'll grow in a day;
Cut them in June,
    That is too soon;
Cut them in July,
    Then they will die.

A Tisket, a Tasket

A tisket, a tasket,
    A green and yellow basket.
I wrote a letter to my love,
    And on the way I dropped it.

I dropped it, I dropped it,
    And on the way I dropped it.
A little girl picked it up
    And put it in her pocket.

The Owl and the Pussycat Went to Sea

The Owl and the Pussycat went to sea
    In a beautiful pea-green boat,
They took some honey, and plenty of money,
    Wrapped up in a five-pound note.

The Owl looked up to the stars above,
    And sang to a small guitar,
"O lovely Pussy! O Pussy, my love,
    What a beautiful Pussy you are,
    You are, you are!
What a beautiful Pussy you are!"

The Coachman

Up at Piccadilly oh!
  The coachman takes his stand,
And when he meets a pretty girl,
  He takes her by the hand;
Whip away for ever oh!
  Drive away so clever oh!
All the way to Bristol oh!
  He drives her four-in-hand.

Feathers

Cackle, cackle, Mother Goose,
  Have you any feathers loose?
Truly have I, pretty fellow,
  Half enough to fill a pillow.
Here are quills, take one or two,
  And down to make a bed for you.

Little Miss Muffet

Little Miss Muffet
  Sat on a tuffet,
Eating her curds and whey;
  There came a big spider,
Who sat down beside her,
  And frightened Miss Muffet away.

Tom, He Was a Piper's Son

Tom, he was a piper's son,
    He learnt to play when he was young,
And all the tune that he could play,
    Was, "Over the hills and far away."

Over the hills and a great way off,
    The wind shall blow my topknot off.

Tom with his pipe made such a noise
    That he pleased both the girls and boys,
And they all stopped to hear him play
    "Over the hills and far away."

Over the hills and a great way off,
    The wind shall blow my topknot off.

Did You See My Wife?

Did you see my wife,
    did you see, did you see,
Did you see my wife
    looking for me?
She wears a straw bonnet,
    with white ribbands on it,
And diminity petticoats
    over her knee.

A Frog He Would a-Wooing Go

A frog he would a-wooing go,
   Heigho! says Rowley,
Whether his mother would let
     him or no,
With a rowley, powley, gammon
   and spinach,
   Heigho! says Rowley.

There Was an Old Man from Peru

There was an old man from Peru
   Who dreamed he was eating
     his shoe.
He woke in a fright
In the middle of the night
   And found it was perfectly true.

Punctuate

Every lady in this land
   Has twenty nails upon each hand.
Five and twenty on hands and feet
   All this is true without deceit.

The Farmer's in His Den

The farmer's in his den,
    The farmer's in his den,
E I E I
    The farmer's in his den.

The farmer wants a wife,
    The farmer wants a wife,
E I E I
    The farmer wants a wife.

The wife wants a child,
    The wife wants a child,
E I E I
    The wife wants a child.

The child wants a nurse,
    The child wants a nurse,
E I E I
    The child wants a nurse.

The nurse wants a dog,
    The nurse wants a dog,
E I E I
    The nurse wants a dog.

We all pat the dog,
    We all pat the dog,
E I E I
    We all pat the dog.

One Man Went to Mow

One man went to mow, went to mow a meadow,
   One man and his dog, Spot,
Went to mow a meadow.

Two men went to mow, went to mow a meadow,
   Two men, one man and his dog, Spot,
Went to mow a meadow.

Three men went to mow, went to mow a meadow,
   Three men, two men, one man and his dog, Spot,
Went to mow a meadow.

Four men went to mow, went to mow a meadow,
   Four men, three men, two men, one man and his dog, Spot,
Went to mow a meadow.

Oranges and Lemons

Oranges and lemons,
    Say the bells of St Clements.
I owe you five farthings,
    Say the bells of St Martins.
When will you pay me?
    Say the bells of Old Bailey.
When I grow rich,
    Say the bells of Shoreditch.

London Bridge is Falling Down

London bridge is falling down,
    Falling down, falling down,
London bridge is falling down,
    My fair lady.

Little Bo-peep

Little Bo-peep has lost her sheep,
    And can't tell where to find them;
Leave them alone, and they'll come home,
    And bring their tails behind them.

Little Bo-peep fell fast asleep,
    And dreamt she heard them bleating;
But when she awoke, she found it a joke,
    For they were still a-fleeting.

Then up she took her little crook,
    Determined for to find them;
She found them indeed, but it made her heart bleed,
    For they'd left all their tails behind ' em.

Jeremiah, Blow the Fire

Jeremiah, blow the fire,
    Puff, puff, puff!
First you blow it gently,
    Then you blow it rough.

Four Wrens

There were two wrens upon a tree,
    Whistle and I'll come to thee;
Another came, and there were three,
    Whistle and I'll come to thee;
Another came and there were four,
    You needn't whistle any more,
For being frightened, off they flew,
    And there are none to show to you.

The Miller of Dee

There was a jolly miller
    Lived on the river Dee:
He worked and sang from morn till night,
    No lark so blithe as he;
And this the burden of his song
    For ever used to be—
I jump mejerrime jee!
    I care for nobody—no! not I,
Since nobody cares for me.

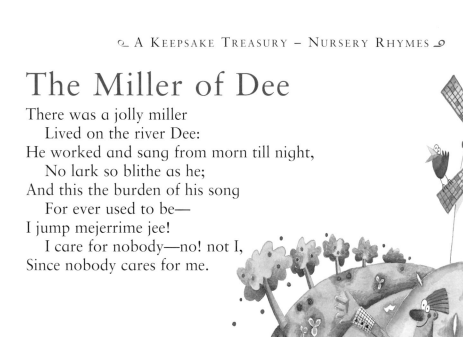

Frère Jacques

Frère Jacques, Frère Jacques,
    Dormez-vous, dormez-vous?
Sonnez les matines,
    Sonnez les matines,
Ding, dang, dong,
    Ding, dang, dong.

Ding, Dong, Bell

Ding, dong, bell,
    Pussy's in the well!
Who put her in?
    Little Tommy Green.
Who pulled her out?
    Little Johnny Stout.
What a naughty boy was that
    To try to drown poor pussy cat,
Who never did any harm,
    But killed the mice in his
        father's barn.

Jack-a-Dandy

Nauty pauty Jack-a-Dandy
    Stole a piece of sugar candy
From the grocer's shoppy shop,
    And away did hoppy-hop.

The Bells of London

Gay go up and gay go down,
    To ring the bells of London town.
Halfpence and farthings,
    Say the bells of St Martin's.
Pancakes and fritters,
    Say the bells of St Peter's.
Two sticks and an apple,
    Say the bells of Whitechapel.

Little Cottage in the Wood

Little cottage in the wood,
    Little old man by the window stood,
Saw a rabbit running by,
    Knocking at the door.
"Help me! Help me! Help me!" he said,
    "Before the huntsman shoots me dead."
"Come little rabbit, come inside,
    Safe with me abide."

Have You Seen the Muffin Man?

Have you seen the muffin man,
    the muffin man, the muffin man,
Have you seen the muffin man that
    lives in Drury Lane O?
Yes, I've seen the muffin man,
    the muffin man, the muffin man;
Yes, I've seen the muffin man who
    lives in Drury Lane O.

Hey de Ho

Hey de, hey de ho,
    The great big elephant
    Is so slow.
Hey de, hey de ho,
    The elephant is so slow.

He swings his tail
    From side to side,
As he takes the children
    For a ride.
Hey de, hey de ho,
    The elephant is so slow.

Hearts, Like Doors

Hearts, like doors, will open with ease
    To very, very, little keys,
And don't forget that two of these
    Are "I thank you" and "If you please".

Willy Boy

Willy boy, Willy boy,
    Where are you going?
I will go with you,
    If that I may.
I'm going to the meadow
    To see them a-mowing,
I am going to help them
    Turn the new hay.

Mother Shuttle

Old Mother Shuttle
    Lived in a coal-scuttle
Along with her dog and her cat;
    What they ate I can't tell,
But 'tis known very well
    That not one of the party was fat.

Gingerbread Men

Smiling girls, rosy boys,
    Come and buy my little toys;
Monkeys made of gingerbread,
    And sugar horses painted red.

There Was a Naughty Boy

There was a naughty boy,
    A naughty boy was he,
He would not stop at home,
    He could not quiet be—
He took
    In his knapsack
A book
    Full of vowels
And a shirt
    With some towels,
A slight cap
    For night cap,
    A hair brush,
    Comb ditto,
    New stockings—
        For old ones
    Would split O!

This knapsack
    Tight at's back
He rivetted close
    And followed his nose
To the North,
    To the North,
And followed his nose
    To the North.

JOHN KEATS

Where are You Going to, My Pretty Maid?

Where are you going to, my pretty maid?
    Where are you going to, my pretty maid?
I'm going a-milking, sir, she said,
    Sir, she said, sir, she said,
I'm going a-milking, sir, she said.

May I go with you, my pretty maid?
    May I go with you, my pretty maid?
You're kindly welcome, sir, she said,
    Sir, she said, sir, she said,
You're kindly welcome, sir, she said.

What is your fortune, my pretty maid?
    What is your fortune, my pretty maid?
My face is my fortune, sir, she said,
    Sir, she said, sir, she said,
My face is my fortune, sir, she said.

Banbury Fair

As I was going to Banbury,
    Upon a summer's day,
My dame had butter, eggs
    and fruit,
    And I had corn and hay.
Joe drove the ox, and Tom
    the swine,
    Dick took the foal and mare;
I sold them all — then home
    to dine,
    From famous Banbury fair.

Then I can't marry you, my pretty maid,
    Then I can't marry you, my pretty maid,
    Nobody asked you, sir, she said,
        Sir, she said, sir, she said,
    Nobody asked you, sir, she said.

The Thaw

Over the land freckled with snow half-thawed
   The speculating rooks at their nests cawed
And saw from elm-tops, delicate as flower of grass,
   What we below could not see, winter pass.

The City Child

Dainty little maiden, whither would you wander?
   Whither from this pretty home, the home where mother dwells?
"Far and far away," said the dainty little maiden,
   "All among the gardens, auriculas, anemones,
Roses and lilies and Canterbury-bells."

Dainty little maiden, whither would you wander?
   Whither from this pretty house, this city house of ours?
"Far and far away," said the dainty little maiden,
   "All among the meadows, the clover and the clematis,
Daisies and kingcups and honeysuckle-flowers."

ALFRED, LORD TENNYSON

The Little Doll

I once had a sweet little doll, dears,
    The prettiest doll in the world;
Her cheeks were so red and so white, dears,
    And her hair was so charmingly curled.
But I lost my poor little doll, dears,
    As I played in the heath one day;
And I cried for her more than a week, dears;
    But I never could find where she lay.

I found my poor little doll, dears,
    As I played in the heath one day:
Folks say she is terribly changed, dears,
    For her paint is all washed away,
And her arm trodden off by the cows, dears,
And her hair not the least bit curled:
Yet for old sakes' sake she is still, dears,
The prettiest doll in the world.

If a Pig Wore a Wig

If a pig wore a wig,
    What could we say?
Treat him as a gentleman,
    And say "Good-day".

If his tail chanced to fail,
    What could we do?
Send him to the tailoress
    To get one new.

CHRISTINA ROSSETTI

Brother and Sister

"Sister, sister go to bed!
    Go and rest your weary head."
Thus the prudent brother said.

"Do you want a battered hide,
    Or scratches to your face applied?"
Thus his sister calm replied.

"Sister, do not raise my wrath.
    I'd make you into mutton broth
As easily as kill a moth!"

The sister raised her beaming eye
    And looked on him indignantly
And sternly answered, "Only try!"

Off to the cook he quickly ran.
    "Dear Cook, please lend a frying-pan
To me as quickly as you can."

"And wherefore should I lend it you?"
    "The reason, Cook, is plain to view.
I wish to make an Irish stew."

"What meat is in that stew to go?"
    "My sister'll be the contents!"
"Oh!"
    "You'll lend the pan to me, Cook?"
        "No!"

Moral: Never stew your sister.

LEWIS CARROLL

Skipping

Little children skip,
　　The rope so gaily gripping,
Tom and Harry,
　　Jane and Mary,
Kate, Diana,
　　Susan, Anna,
All are fond of skipping!

The little boats they skip,
　　Beside the heavy shipping,
And while the squalling
　　Winds are calling,
Falling, rising,
　　Rising, falling
All are fond of skipping!

The Mad Gardener's Song

He thought he saw an Elephant,
　　That practised on a fife:
He looked again, and found it was
　　A letter from his wife.
"At length I realize," he said,
　　"The bitterness of Life!"

He thought he saw a Banker's Clerk
　　Descending from the bus:
He looked again, and found it was
　　A Hippopotamus:
"If this should stay to dine," he said,
　　"There won't be much for us!"

Minnie and Winnie

Minnie and Winnie
Slept in a shell.
Sleep, little ladies!
And they slept well.

Pink was the shell within,
Silver without;
Sounds of the great sea
Wandered about.

Sleep, little ladies,
Wake not soon!
Echo on echo
Dies to the moon.

Two bright stars
Peeped into the shell.
"What are they dreaming of?
Who can tell?"

Started a green linnet
Out of the croft;
Wake, little ladies,
The sun is aloft!

ALFRED, LORD TENNYSON

Night-light

You've no need to light a night-light
On a light night like tonight,
For a night-light's light's a slight light,
And tonight's a night that's light.
When a night's light, like tonight's light,
It is really not quite right
To light night-lights with their slight lights
On a light night like tonight.

A Boy's Song

Where the pools are bright and deep,
   Where the gray trout lies asleep,
Up the river and o'er the lea,
   That's the way for Billy and me.

Where the blackbird sings the latest,
   Where the hawthorn blooms the sweetest,
Where the nestlings chirp and flee,
   That's the way for Billy and me.

Where the mowers mow the cleanest,
   Where the hay lies thick and greenest;
There to trace the homeward bee,
   That's the way for Billy and me.

Why the boys should drive away
   Little sweet maidens from their play,
Or love the banter and fight so well,
   That's the thing I never could tell.

But this I know, I love to play
   Through the meadow, among the hay;
Up the water and o'er the lea,
   That's the way for Billy and me.

Minnie and Mattie

Minnie and Mattie
    And fat little May,
Out in the country,
    Spending a day.

Such a bright day,
    With the sun glowing,
And the trees half in leaf,
    And the grass growing.

Minnie and Mattie
    And May carry posies,
Half of sweet violets,
    Half of primroses.

Give the sun time enough,
    Glowing and glowing,
He'll rouse the roses
    And bring them blowing.

Violets and primroses
    Blossom to-day
For Minnie and Mattie
    And fat little May.

CHRISTINA ROSSETTI

Hey, Diddle, Diddle

Hey, diddle, diddle, the cat and the fiddle,
    The cow jumped over the moon;
The little dog laughed to see such sport,
    And the dish ran away with the spoon!

The Swing

How do you like to go up in a swing,
    Up in the air so blue?
Oh, I do think it the pleasantest thing
    Ever a child can do!

Up in the air and over the wall,
    Till I can see so wide,
Rivers and trees and cattle and all
    Over the countryside —

Till I look down on the garden green,
    Down on the roof so brown —
Up in the air I go flying again,
    Up in the air and down!

ROBERT LOUIS STEVENSON

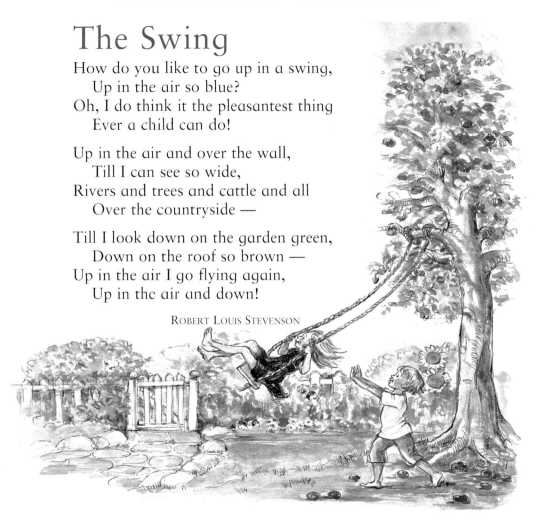

There Was an Old Man With a Beard

There was an old Man with a beard,
  Who said, "It is just as I feared! —
Two Owls and a Hen, four Larks and a Wren
  Have all built their nests in my beard!"

EDWARD LEAR

A Bitter Bittern

A bitter biting bittern
  Bit a better brother bittern,
And the bitter better bittern
  Bit the bitter biter back.
And the bitter bittern, bitten,
  By the better bitten bittern,
Said: "I'm a bitter biter bit, alack!"

Bread and Milk for Breakfast

Bread and milk for breakfast,
  And woollen frocks to wear,
And a crumb for robin redbreast
  On the cold days of the year.

CHRISTINA ROSSETTI

All the Bells Were Ringing

All the bells were ringing
    And all the birds were singing,
When Molly sat down crying
    For her broken doll.

O you silly Moll!
    Sobbing and sighing
    For a broken doll,
When all the bells are ringing
    And all the birds are singing.

CHRISTINA ROSSETTI

How Much Wood?

How much wood
would a woodchuck chuck if a
woodchuck could chuck wood?
He would chuck, he would, as much
as he could, and chuck as much wood
as a woodchuck would if a
woodchuck could chuck wood.

Hurt No Living Thing

Hurt no living thing,
    Ladybird nor butterfly,
Nor moth with dusty wing,
Nor cricket chirping cheerily,
Nor grasshopper, so light of leap,
    Nor dancing gnat,
    Nor beetle fat,
Nor harmless worms that creep.

CHRISTINA ROSSETTI

Donkey Riding

Were you ever in Quebec,
Stowing timbers on a deck,
Where there's a king in his golden
crown
Riding on a donkey?

Hey ho, and away we go,
Donkey riding, donkey riding,
Hey ho, and away we go,
Riding on a donkey.

Were you ever in Cardiff Bay,
Where the folks all shout, Hooray!
Here comes John with his three
months' pay,
Riding on a donkey?

Hey ho, and away we go,
Donkey riding, donkey riding,
Hey ho, and away we go,
Riding on a donkey.

Were you ever off Cape Horn,
Where it's always fine and
warm?
See the lion and the unicorn
Riding on a donkey.

Hey ho, and away we go,
Donkey riding, donkey riding,
Hey ho, and away we go,
Riding on a donkey.

Going Down Hill on a Bicycle

With lifted feet, hands still,
    I am poised, and down the hill
Dart, with heedful mind;
    The air goes by in a wind.

Swifter and yet more swift,
    Till the heart with a mighty lift
Makes the lungs laugh, the throat cry:—
    "O bird, see; see, bird, I fly.

"Is this, is this your joy?
    O bird, then I, though a boy,
For a golden moment share
    Your feathery life in air!"

Say, heart, is there aught like this
    In a world that is full of bliss?
'Tis more than skating, bound
    Steel-shod to the level ground.

Speed slackens now, I float
    Awhile in my airy boat;
Till, when the wheels scarce crawl,
    My feet to the treadles fall.

Alas, that the longest hill
    Must end in a vale; but still,
Who climbs with toil, wheresoe'er,
    Shall find wings waiting there.

HENRY CHARLES BEECHING

The Walrus and the Carpenter

"The time has come," the Walrus said,
    "To talk of many things:
Of shoes—and ships—and sealing-wax—
    Of cabbages—and kings—
And why the sea is boiling hot—
    And whether pigs have wings."

"But wait a bit," the Oysters cried,
    "Before we have our chat;
For some of us are out of breath,
    And all of us are fat!"
"No hurry!" said the carpenter.
    They thanked him much for that.

"A load of bread," the Walrus said,
    "Is what we chiefly need:
Pepper and vinegar besides
    Are very good indeed—
Now if you're ready, Oysters dear,
    We can begin to feed."

LEWIS CARROLL

Autumn Fires

In the other gardens
    And all up the vale,
From the autumn bonfires
    See the smoke trail!

Pleasant summer over
    And all the summer flowers,
The red fire blazes,
    The grey smoke towers.

Sing a song of seasons!
    Something bright in all!
Flowers in the summer,
    Fires in the fall!

ROBERT LOUIS STEVENSON

Ariel's Song

Full fathom five thy father lies;
Of his bones are coral made;
Those are pearls that were his eyes:
Nothing of him that doth fade,
But doth suffer a sea-change
Into something rich and strange:
Sea nymphs hourly ring his knell.
Ding-dong!
Hark! now I hear them,
Ding-dong, bell!

There's a Hole in the Middle of the Sea

There's a hole, there's a hole,
   there's a hole in the middle of the sea.
There's a log in the hole in the middle
   of the sea.
There's a hole, there's a hole,
   there's a hole in the middle of the sea.
There's a bump on the log in the
   hole in the middle of the sea.
There's a hole, there's a hole,
   there's a hole in the middle of the sea.

There's a frog on the bump on the
   log in the hole in the middle of
    the sea.
There's a hole, there's a hole, there's
   a hole in the middle of the sea.
There's a fly on the frog on the bump
   on the log in the hole in the middle
    of the sea.
There's a hole, there's a hole, there's
   a hole in the middle of the sea.

The Children's Hour

Between the dark and the daylight,
    When the night is beginning to lower,
Comes a pause in the day's occupations,
    That is known as the Children's Hour.

I hear in the chamber above me
    The patter of little feet,
The sound of a door that is opened,
    And voices soft and sweet.

From my study I see in the lamplight,
    Descending the broad hall stair,
Grave Alice, and laughing Allegra,
    And Edith with golden hair.

A whisper, and then a silence:
    Yet I know by their merry eyes
They are plotting and planning together
    To take me by surprise.

Happy Thought

The world is so full
    of a number of things,
I'm sure we should all be
    as happy as kings.

Spring

Sound the Flute!
  Now it's mute.
Birds delight
  Day and Night;
Nightingale
  In the dale,
Lark in Sky,
  Merrily,
Merrily, Merrily, to
  welcome in the Year.

Little Boy,
  Full of joy;
Little Girl,
  Sweet and small;
Cock does crow,
  So do you;
Merry voice,
  Infant noise,
Merrily, Merrily, to
  welcome in the Year.

WILLIAM BLAKE

Old King Cole

Old King Cole
  Was a merry old soul,
And a merry old soul was he;
  He called for his pipe,
And he called for his bowl,
  And he called for his fiddlers three.
Every fiddler had a fine fiddle,
  And a very fine fiddle had he;
Twee tweedle dee, tweedle dee, went the
    fiddlers three,
  Oh there's none so rare
  As can compare
With King Cole and his fiddlers three.

Two Little Kittens

Two little kittens
   One stormy night,
Began to quarrel,
   And then to fight.

One had a mouse
   And the other had none;
And that was the way
   The quarrel begun.

"I'll have that mouse,"
   Said the bigger cat.
"You'll have that mouse?
   We'll see about that!"

"I will have that mouse,"
   Said the tortoise-shell;
And, spitting and
     scratching,
   On her sister she fell.

I've told you before
   'Twas a stormy night,
When these two kittens
   Began to fight.

The old woman took
   The sweeping broom,
And swept them both
   Right out of the room.

The ground was covered
   With frost and snow,
They had lost the mouse,
   And had nowhere to go.

So they lay and shivered
   Beside the door,
Till the old woman finished
   Sweeping the floor.

And then they crept in
   As quiet as mice,
All wet with snow
   And as cold as ice.

They found it much better
   That stormy night,
To lie by the fire,
   Than to quarrel and fight.

JANE TAYLOR

Humpty Dumpty's Poem

In winter, when the fields are white,
    I sing this song for your delight —
In spring, when woods are getting green,
    I'll try and tell you what I mean.
In summer, when the days are long,
    Perhaps you'll understand the song:
In autumn, when the leaves are brown,
    Take pen and ink, and write it down.

I sent a message to the fish:
    I told them "This is what I wish."
The little fishes of the sea,
    They sent an answer back to me.
The little fishes' answer was
    "We cannot do it, Sir, because — "
I sent to them again to say
    "It will be better to obey."

Round and Round the Garden

Round and round the garden,
    Like a teddy bear.
One step, two steps,
    Tickly under there!

Round and round the haystack,
    Went the little mouse.
One step, two steps,
    In this little house.

Frog Went a-Courtin'

Mr Froggie went a-courtin' an' he did ride;
  Sword and pistol by his side.
He went to Missus Mousie's hall,
  Gave a loud knock and gave a loud call.

"Pray, Missus Mousie, air you within?"
  "Yes, kind sir, I set an' spin."
He tuk Miss Mousie on his knee,
  An' sez, "Miss Mousie, will ya marry me?"

Dingle Dangle Scarecrow

When all the cows were sleeping
  And the sun had gone to bed,
Up jumped the scarecrow
  And this is what he said:

I'm a dingle dangle scarecrow
  With a flippy floppy hat!
I can shake my arms like this,
  I can shake my legs like that!

When the cows were in the meadow
  And the pigeons in the loft,
Up jumped the scarecrow
  And whispered very soft:
Chorus

When all the hens were roosting
  And the moon behind a cloud,
Up jumped the scarecrow
  And shouted very loud:
Chorus

Welcome Little Chick

With a scritch and a scratch and
    tippity tap,
  The shiny shell begins to crack.
A hole appears and then a beak,
  Two beady eyes now take a peek.

A head peeps through, it
starts to shout.
    It wiggles and wiggles, and
      yells, "Let me out!"
He fluffs up his feathers
    and gives a big kick.
The shell breaks in two
    and there is a chick!

The Noisy Farm

Chicks and ducks and geese and hens,
  Pigs and cows and sheep,
Shouting OINK and MOO and CLUCK,
HONK and BAA and CHEEP!

Down on Primrose Farm each day,
  Horses neigh and donkeys bray.
It's really such a noisy place,
  Till Mr Sunshine hides his face.
Then they snore and snooze and yawn,
  Until the rooster crows, "It's dawn!"

Happy Hatching Days

Chicks are here,
  Chicks are there,
Chicks are hatching everywhere!
  Poking out their tiny beaks,
They open wide and call,
  "Cheep! Cheep!"

So, is this a special day,
  When all the chicks come out
    to play?
Yes, it is! Hip, hip hooray!
  At last, it's Happy
    Hatching Day!

Second-hand Bear

He had one tattered ear
And he had lost his squeak.
He looked so very shabby,
Oh, and yes, he couldn't speak.

His fur was worn and patchy.
He only had one eye.
There were a lot of other toys
In there that I could buy.

But he seemed so very tearful,
On the shelf all alone.
It looked like he was longing
For a best friend of his own.

So I took him home to my house
And I tried to fix his eye.
I put a patch upon his ear,
And now I'll tell you why.

I knew that all he needed
Was a little bit of care,
And I had fallen quite in love
With that second-hand old bear.

If All the Seas Were One Sea

If all the seas were one sea,
    What a great sea that would be!
And if all the trees were one tree,
    What a great tree that would be!
And if all the axs were one ax,
    What a great ax that would be!

And if all the men were one man,
    What a great man he would be!
And if the great man took the great ax,
    And cut down the great tree,
And let it fall into the great sea,
    What a splish splash that would be!

If You're Happy and You Know It

If you're happy and you know it,
    Clap your hands.
If you're happy and you know it,
    Clap your hands.
If you're happy and you know it,
    And you really want to show it,
    If you're happy and
        you know it,
        Clap your hands.

If you're happy and you know it,
    Nod your head, etc.

If you're happy and you know it,
    Stamp your feet, etc.

If you're happy and you know it,
    Say "ha, ha!", etc.

If you're happy and you know it,
    Do all four!

Cock Robin's Courtship

Cock Robin got up early
  At the break of day,
And went to Jenny's window
  To sing a roundelay.
He sang Cock Robin's love
  To little Jenny Wren,
And when he got unto the end
  Then he began again.

The Girl in the Lane

The girl in the lane,
  That couldn't speak plain,
Cried, "Gobble, gobble, gobble."
The man on the hill,
  That couldn't stand still,
Went hobble, hobble, hobble.

Engine, Engine

Engine, engine, number nine,
  Sliding down Chicago line;
When she's polished she will shine,
  Engine, engine, number nine.

Old Farmer Giles

Old Farmer Giles,
  He went seven miles
With his faithful dog Old Rover;
  And Old Farmer Giles,
When he came to the stiles,
  Took a run, and jumped clean over.

Against Quarrelling and Fighting

Let dogs delight to bark and bite,
    For God hath made them so:
Let bears and lions growl and fight,
    For 'tis their nature, too.

But, children, you should never let
    Such angry passions rise:
Your little hands were never made
    To tear each other's eyes.

Let love through all your actions run,
    And all your words be mild:
Live like the blessed Virgin's Son,
    That sweet and lovely child.

His soul was gentle as a lamb;
    And as his nature grew,
He grew in favour both with man,
    And God his Father, too.

Now, Lord of all, he reigns above,
    And from his heavenly throne
He sees what children dwell in love,
    And marks them for his own.

Little Fishes

Little fishes in a brook,
    Father caught them on a hook,
Mother fried them in a pan,
    Johnnie eats them like a man.

Little Things

Little drops of water,
 Little grains of sand,
Make the mighty ocean
 And the beauteous land.

And the little moments,
 Humble though they be,
Make the mighty ages
 Of eternity.

One, Two

One, two, whatever you do,
 Start it well and carry it through.
Try, try, never say die,
 Things will come right,
 You know, by and by.

So our little errors
 Lead the soul away,
From the paths of virtue
 Into sin to stray.

Little deeds of kindness,
 Little words of love,
Make our earth an Eden,
 Like the heaven above.

Pussycat, Pussycat

Pussycat, pussycat, where have you been?
 I've been to London to visit the Queen.
Pussycat, pussycat, what did you there?
 I frightened a little mouse under her chair.

I Sell You the Key of the King's Garden

I sell you the key of the King's garden:
    I sell you the string that ties the key of the King's garden:
I sell you the rat that gnawed the string that ties the key of
    the King's garden:
I sell you the cat that caught the rat that gnawed the string that ties
    the key of the King's garden:
I sell you the dog that bit the cat that caught the rat that gnawed the
    string that ties the key of the King's garden.

If All the World Was Apple-pie

If all the world was apple-pie,
    And all the sea was ink,
And all the trees were bread and cheese,
    What should we have for drink?

The Broom Song

Here's a large one for the lady,
  Here's a small one for the baby;
Come buy, my pretty lady,
  Come buy o' me a broom.

Thank You

Thank you for your portrait,
  I think it's very nice.
I've put it in the attic
  To scare away the mice.

There Was An Old Woman Called Nothing-at-all

There was an old woman called Nothing-at-all,
  Who rejoiced in a dwelling exceedingly small;
A man stretched his mouth to its utmost extent,
  And down at one gulp house and old woman went.

Washing Day

The old woman must stand
  At the tub, tub, tub,
  The dirty clothes to rub, rub, rub;
But when they are clean,
  And fit to be seen,
She'll dress like a lady
  And dance on the green.

My Maid Mary

My maid Mary,
   She minds the dairy,
While I go a-hoeing and mowing each morn;
   Merrily runs the reel,
   And the little spinning wheel,
Whilst I am singing and mowing my corn.

Firefly, Firefly

Firefly, firefly, yellow and bright
   Bridle the filly under your light,
The son of the king is ready to ride,
   Firefly, firefly, fly by my side.

Hector Protector

Hector Protector was dressed all in green;
   Hector Protector was sent to the Queen.
The Queen did not like him, nor more did
    the King;
So Hector Protector was sent back again.

Wagtail and Baby

A blaring bull went wading through,
   The wagtail showed no shrinking.

A stallion splashed his way across,
   The birdie nearly sinking;
He gave his plumes a twitch and toss,
   And held his own unblinking.

Next saw the baby round the spot
   A mongrel slowing slinking;
The wagtail gazed, but faltered not
   In dip and sip and prinking.

A perfect gentleman then neared;
   The wagtail, in a winking,
With terror rose and disappeared;
   The baby fell a-thinking.

See-saw,
Margery Daw

See-saw, Margery Daw,
   Johnny shall have a new master;
He shall have but a penny a day,
   Because he can't work any faster.

The Man in the Wilderness

The man in the wilderness asked me,
How many strawberries grew in the sea?
I answered him as I thought good,
As many red herrings as grew in the wood.

Leg Over Leg

Leg over leg,
As the dog went to Dover;
When he came to a stile,
Jump he went over.

The Gossips

Miss One, Two, and Three
Could never agree,
While they gossiped around
A tea-caddy.

Puss at the Door

Who's that ringing at my door bell?
A little pussy cat that isn't very well.
Rub its little nose with a little mutton fat,
That's the best cure for a little pussy cat.

As I Walked by Myself

As I walked by myself,
    And talked to myself,
Myself said unto me,
    Look to thyself,
Take care of thyself,
    For nobody cares for thee.

I answered myself,
    And said to myself,
In the self-same repartee,
    Look to thyself,
Or not look to thyself,
    The self-same thing will be.

The Dove Says

The dove says,
    Coo, coo,
What shall I do?
    I can scarce maintain two.
Pooh, pooh, says the wren, I have ten,
    And keep them all like gentlemen.
Curr dhoo, curr dhoo,
    Love me, and I'll love you.

Tommy Trot

Tommy Trot,
    a man of law,
Sold his bed and
    lay upon straw:
Sold the straw and
    slept on grass,
To buy his wife
    a looking-glass.

Simple Gifts

'Tis the gift to be simple,
  'Tis the gift to be free,
'Tis the gift to come down
  Where we ought to be,
And when we find ourselves
  In the place just right,
'Twill be in the valley
  Of love and delight.
When true simplicity is gained
To bow and to bend
  We sha'n't be ashamed,
To turn, turn will be our delight,
Till by turning, turning
  We come round right.

Charley Barley

Charley Barley, butter and eggs,
  Sold his wife for three duck eggs.
When the ducks began to lay,
  Charley Barley flew away.

Dibbity, Dibbity, Dibbity, Doe

Dibbity, dibbity, dibbity, doe,
  Give me a pancake
  And I'll go.
Dibbity, dibbity, dibbity,
    ditter,
Please to give me
  A bit of a fritter.

Yankee Doodle

Yankee Doodle came to town,
   A-ridin' on a pony;
He stuck a feather in his hat;
   And called it macaroni.

Yankee Doodle keep it up,
   Yankee Doodle Dandy;
Mind the music and the steps
   And with the girls be handy.

Father and I went down to camp.
   Along with Cap'n Goodwin;
The men and boys all stood around
   As thick as hasty puddin'.

Yankee Doodle keep it up,
   Yankee Doodle Dandy;
Mind the music and the steps
   And with the girls be handy.

Fidget

As little Jenny Wren
   Was sitting by the shed,
She waggled with her tail,
   She nodded with her head;
She waggled with her tail,
   She nodded with her head;
As Little Jenny Wren
   Was sitting by the shed.

Buff

I had a dog
   Whose name was Buff,
I sent him for
   A bag of snuff;
He broke the bag
   And spilt the stuff,
And that was all
   My penny's worth.

Lazy Mary

Lazy Mary will you get up,
  Will you get up, will you get up?
Lazy Mary will you get up,
  Will you get up today?

Six o'clock and you're still sleeping,
  Daylight's creeping o'er your
    windowsill.

Lazy Mary will you get up,
  Will you get up, will you get up?
Lazy Mary will you get up,
  Will you get up today?

Seven o'clock and you're still snoring,
  Sunshine's pouring through your
    window pane.

Lazy Mary will you get up,
  Will you get up, will you get up?
Lazy Mary will you get up,
  Will you get up today?

Eight o'clock, you've missed your train,
  Can you explain why you're still
    in your bed?

Silly Sally

Silly Sally swiftly shooed seven
  silly sheep.
The seven silly sheep Silly Sally
  shooed shilly-shallied south.
These sheep shouldn't sleep in a
  shack; sheep should sleep in
  a shed.

Betty Pringle

Betty Pringle had a little pig,
   Not very little and not very big;
When he was alive he lived in clover;
   But now he's dead, and that's all over.
So Billy Pringle, he laid down and cried,
And Betty Pringle, she laid down
     and died;
So there was an end of one,
     two, and three:
   Billy Pringle he,
     Betty Pringle she,
And the piggy wiggy.

Ten Little Men

Ten little men standing straight,
   Ten little men open the gate,
Ten little men all in a ring,
Ten little men bow to the king,
   Ten little men dance all day,
Ten little men hide away.

The Queen of Hearts

The Queen of Hearts, she made some tarts,
   All on a summer's day;
The Knave of Hearts, he stole the tarts,
   And took them clean away.

The King of Hearts called for the tarts,
   And beat the Knave full sore;
The Knave of Hearts brought back the tarts,
   And vowed he'd steal no more.

In the Dark, Dark Wood

In the dark, dark wood, there was a dark, dark house,
And in that dark, dark house, there was a dark, dark room,
And in that dark, dark room, there was a dark, dark cupboard,
And in that dark, dark cupboard, there was a dark, dark shelf,
And on that dark, dark shelf, there was a dark, dark box,
And in that dark, dark box, there was a

GHOST!

Bobbie Shaftoe

Bobbie Shaftoe's gone to sea,
Silver buckles at his knee;
When he comes back
He'll marry me,
Bonny Bobbie Shaftoe!

At the Siege of Belle-isle

At the siege of Belle-isle, I was there all the while,
All the while, all the while, at the siege of Belle-isle.

When I Was a Bachelor

When I was a bachelor I lived by myself,
  And all the meat I got I put upon a shelf;
The rats and the mice did lead me such a life
  That I went to London to get myself a wife.

The streets were so broad and the lanes were so narrow,
  I could not get my wife home without a wheelbarrow;
The wheelbarrow broke, my wife got a fall,
  Down tumbled wheelbarrow, little wife, and all.

When Jacky's a Very Good Boy

When Jacky's a very good boy,
  He shall have cakes and a custard;
But when he does nothing but cry,
  He shall have nothing but mustard.

Little Betty Blue

Little Betty Blue
Lost a holiday shoe,
    What can little Betty do?
Give her another
To match the other,
    And then she may
        swagger in two.

Cuckoo, Cuckoo

Cuckoo, Cuckoo,
    What do you do?
In April
    I open my bill;
In May
    I sing night and day;
In June
    I change my tune;
In July
    Away I fly;
In August
    Away I must.

Miss Mary Mack

Miss Mary Mack, Mack, Mack,
    All dressed in black, black, black,
With silver buttons, buttons, buttons,
    All down her back, back, back.
She went upstairs to make her bed,
    She made a mistake and bumped her head;
She went downstairs to wash the dishes,
    She made a mistake and washed her wishes;
She went outside to hang her clothes,
    She made a mistake and hung her nose.

The World

Great, wide, beautiful, wonderful World,
    With the wonderful water round you curled,
And the wonderful grass upon your breast—
    World, you are beautifully dressed.

The wonderful air is over me,
    And the wonderful wind is shaking the tree,
It walks on the water, and whirls the mills,
    And talks to itself on the tops of the hills.

You friendly Earth, how far do you go,
    With the wheatfields that nod and the rivers that flow,
With cities and gardens, and cliffs, and isles,
    And people upon you for thousands of miles?

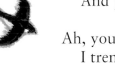

Ah, you are so great, and I am so small,
    I tremble to think of you, World, at all;
And yet, when I said my prayers today,
    A whisper inside me seemed to say,
"You are more than the Earth, though you are such a dot:
    You can love and think, and the Earth cannot."

WILLIAM BRIGHTY RANDS

Snow

In the gloom of whiteness,
　　In the great silence of snow,
A child was sighing
　　And bitterly saying: "Oh,
They have killed a white bird up there
　　　　on her nest,
　　The down is fluttering from her breast!"
And still it fell through that dusky
　　　　brightness
　　On the child crying for the bird of
　　　　the snow.

EDWARD THOMAS

Little Tommy Tucker

Little Tommy Tucker
   Sings for his supper:
What shall we give him?
   Brown bread and butter.
How shall he cut it
   Without a knife?
How can he marry
   Without a wife?

A Sailor Went to Sea, Sea, Sea

A sailor went to sea, sea, sea,
   To see what he could see, see, see,
But all that he could see, see, see,
   Was the bottom of the deep blue
     sea, sea, sea.

There Was a Little Boy

There was a little boy went into a barn,
    And lay down on some hay;
An owl came out and flew about,
    And the little boy ran away.

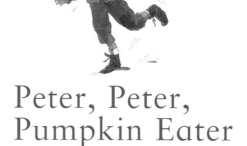

And That's All

There was an old man,
And he had a calf,
    And that's half;
He took him out of the stall,
And put him on the wall,
    And that's all.

Peter, Peter, Pumpkin Eater

Peter, Peter, pumpkin eater,
    Had a wife and couldn't keep her;
He put her in a pumpkin shell
    And there he kept her very well.

Peter, Peter, pumpkin eater,
    Had another and didn't love her;
Peter learned to read and spell,
    And then he loved her very well.

Johnny Shall Have a New Bonnet

Johnny shall have a new bonnet,
    And Johnny shall go to the fair,
And Johnny shall have a blue ribbon
    To tie up his bonny brown hair.

Simple Simon

Simple Simon met a pieman
    Going to the fair;
Said Simple Simon to the pieman,
    "Let me taste your ware."

Said the pieman to Simple Simon,
    "Show me first your penny";
Said Simple Simon to the pieman,
    "Indeed I have not any."

The Little Rusty, Dusty Miller

O the little rusty, dusty miller,
Dusty was his coat,
    Dusty was his colour,
Dusty was the kiss
    I got from the miller.
If I had my pockets
    Full of gold and silver,
I would give it all
    To my dusty miller.

The Wheels on the Bus

The wheels on the bus go round and round,
  Round and round, round and round,
The wheels on the bus go round and round,
  All day long.

The wipers on the bus go swish, swish, swish,
  Swish, swish, swish, swish, swish, swish,
The wipers on the bus go swish, swish, swish,
  All day long.

The horn on the bus goes beep! beep! beep!
  Beep! beep! beep! beep! beep! beep!
The horn on the bus goes beep! beep! beep!
  All day long.

The people on the bus go chat, chat, chat,
  Chat, chat, chat, chat, chat, chat,
The people on the bus go chat, chat, chat,
  All day long.

The children on the bus bump up and down,
  Up and down, up and down,
The children on the bus bump up and down,
  All day long.

To the Magpie

Magpie, magpie, flutter
  and flee,
Turn up your tail and
  good luck come to me.

Rain

Rain before seven,
  Fine by eleven.

I Had a Little Hobby Horse

I had a little hobby horse, it was well shod,
    It carried me to London, niddety nod,
And when we got to London we heard a great shout,
    Down fell my hobby horse and I cried out:
"Up again, hobby horse, if thou be a beast,
    When we get to our town we will have a feast,
And if there be but a little, why thou shall have some,
    And dance to the bag-pipes and beating of the drum."

Billy and Me

One, two, three,
    I love coffee,
And Billy loves tea,
    How good you be,
One two three,
    I love coffee,
And Billy loves tea.

Here Comes a Widow

Here comes a widow from Barbary-land,
    With all her children in her hand;
One can brew, and one can bake,
    And one can make a wedding-cake.
Pray take one, pray take two,
    Pray take one that pleases you.

Elsie Marley

Elsie Marley is grown so fine,
    She won't get up to serve the
But lies in bed till eight or nine,
    And surely she does take her

I Love Thee, Betty

I love thee, Betty,
    Do'st thou, Johnny?
Hey, but I wonder where!
    In my heart, Betty.
In thy heart, Johnny?
    Thou never made it appear.

But I'll wed thee, Betty.
    Wed me, Johnny?
Hey, but I wonder when!
    On Sunday, Betty.
On Sunday, Johnny?
    Hey, I wish it was Sunday then.

Lucy Locket

Lucy Locket lost her pocket,
    Kitty Fisher found it.
Not a penny was there in it,
    Only ribbon round it.

Cinderella's umbrella's
    Full of holes all over.
Every time it starts to rain
    She has to run for cover.

Aladdin's lamp is getting damp,
    And is no longer gleaming.
It doesn't spark within the dark,
    But you can't stop it steaming.

There was a Little Boy

There was a little boy and a little girl.
    Lived in an alley;
Says the little boy to the little girl,
    "Shall I, oh, shall I?"

Says the little girl to the little boy,
    "What shall we do?"
Says the little boy to the little girl,
    "I will kiss you."

Warning

The robin and the redbreast,
    The robin and the wren:
If you takes from their nest
    You'll never thrive again.

Cobbler, Cobbler

Cobbler, cobbler, mend my shoe,
    Get it done by half past two;
Stitch it up, and stitch it down,
    Then I'll give you half a crown.

One-ery, You-ery

One-ery, you-ery, ekery, Ann,
    Phillisy, follysy, Nicholas, John,
Quee-bee, quaw-bee, Irish Mary,
    Stinkle-em, stankle-em, buck.

Here is the Church

Here is the church,
    Here is the steeple,
Open the doors,
    And here are the people.
Here is the parson, going upstairs,
    And here he is a-saying his prayers.

What's the News of the Day

What's the news of the day,
    Good neighbor, I pray?
They say the balloon
    Is gone up to the moon.

Chairs to Mend

If I'd as much money as I could spend,
    I never would cry, "Old chairs to mend.
Old chairs to mend! Old chairs to mend!"
    I never would cry, "Old chairs to mend!"

A Squabble

Moll-in-the-Wad and I fell out,
    What do you think it was all about?
I gave her a shilling, she swore it was bad,
    It's an old soldier's button, says Moll-in-the-Wad.

Epigram

*Engraved on the Collar of a Dog
which I Gave to His Royal Highness*
I am his Highness' Dog at Kew:
Pray tell me, sir, whose dog are you?

ALEXANDER POPE

Tommy Snooks and Bessy Brooks

As Tommy Snooks and Bessy Brooks
   Were walking out one Sunday.
Says Tommy Snooks to Bessy Brooks,
   "Tomorrow will be Monday."

Three Little Ghostesses

Three little ghostesses,
   Sitting on postesses,
Eating buttered toastesses,
   Greasing their fistesses,
Up to their wristesses.
   Oh what beastesses
To make such feastesses!

The Giant

Fee, fi, fo, fum,
   I smell the blood
      of an Englishman:
Be he alive or be he dead,
   I'll grind his bones to
      make my bread.

Answers to a Child's Question

Do you ask what the birds say? The sparrow, the dove,
    The linnet and thrush say, "I love and I love!"
In the winter they're silent, the wind is so strong;
    What it says I don't know, but it sings a loud song.
But green leaves, and blossoms, and sunny warm weather,
    And singing and loving—all come back together.
But the lark is so brimful of gladness and love,
    The green fields below him, the blue sky above,
That he sings, and he sings, and for ever sings he,
    "I love my Love, and my Love loves me."

SAMUEL TAYLOR COLERIDGE

Dance to Your Daddy

Dance to your daddy,
  My little babby;
Dance to your daddy,
  My little lamb.

You shall have a fishy,
  In a little dishy;
You shall have a fishy
  When the boat comes in.

The Cat of Cats

I am the cat of cats. I am
  The everlasting cat!
Cunning, and old, and sleek as jam,
  The everlasting cat!
I hunt the vermin in the night—
  The everlasting cat!
For I see best without the light—
  The everlasting cat!

Puss in the Pantry

Hie, hie, says Anthony,
  Puss is in the pantry,
Gnawing, gnawing,
  A mutton, mutton bone;
See how she tumbles it,
  See how she mumbles it,
See how she tosses
  The mutton, mutton bone.

The Squirrel

The winds they did blow,
　　The leaves they did wag;
Along came a beggar boy,
　　And put me in his bag.

He took me to London,
　　A lady me did buy,
Put me in a silver cage,
　　And hung me up on high.

With apples by the fire,
　　And nuts for me to crack,
Besides a little feather bed
　　To rest my little back.

Tickly, Tickly

Tickly, tickly, on your knee,
　　If you laugh, you don't love me.

One, Two, Three, Four, Five

One, two, three, four, five,
　　Once I caught a fish alive;
Six, seven, eight, nine, ten,
　　Then I let him go again.
Why did you let him go?
　　Because he bit my finger so.
Which finger did he bite?
　　This little finger on the right.

Windy Nights

Whenever the moon and stars are set,
　　Whenever the wind is high,
All night long in the dark and wet,
　　A man goes riding by.
Late in the night when the fires are out,
　　Why does he gallop and gallop about?

Whenever the trees are crying aloud,
　　And ships are tossed at sea,
By, on the highway, low and loud,
　　By at the gallop goes he.
But at the gallop he goes, and then
By he comes back at the gallop again.

ROBERT LOUIS STEVENSON

Pitter-patter

Pitter-patter,
　　Pitter-patter
Listen to the rain!
Pitter-patter,
　　Pitter-patter,
On the window pane!

The Key of the Kingdom

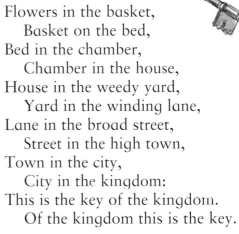

This is the key of the kingdom:
In that kingdom is a city,
  In that city is a town,
In that town there is a street,
  In that street there winds a lane,
In that lane there is a yard,
  In that yard there is a house,
In that house there waits a room,
  In that room there is a bed,
On that bed there is a basket,
  A basket of flowers.

Flowers in the basket,
  Basket on the bed,
Bed in the chamber,
  Chamber in the house,
House in the weedy yard,
  Yard in the winding lane,
Lane in the broad street,
  Street in the high town,
Town in the city,
  City in the kingdom:
This is the key of the kingdom.
  Of the kingdom this is the key.

To Sleep Easy
At Night

To sleep easy at night.
  Let your supper be light,
Or else you'll complain
  Of a stomach pain.

For Every Evil Under the Sun

For every evil under the sun,
    There is a remedy, or there is none.
If there be one, try and find it;
    If there be none, never mind it.

There Was a King and he Had Three Daughters

There was a king,
    And he had three daughters,
And they all lived,
    In a basin of water;
The basin bended,
    My story's ended.
If the basin had been stronger,
    My story would be longer.

Flee from fog to fight flu fast!

Nine nice night nurses nursing nicely.

Sam's shop stocks short spotted socks.

Shy Shelly says she shall sew sheets.

Tim, the thin twin tinsmith.

This Little Froggy

This little froggy took a big leap,
   This little froggy took a small,
This little froggy leaped sideways,
   And this little froggy not at all,
And this little froggy went,
   Hippity, hippity, hippity hop, all the way home.

I Am a Gold Lock

I am a gold lock.
   I am a gold key.
I am a silver lock.
   I am a silver key.

I am a brass lock.
   I am a brass key.
I am a lead lock.
   I am a lead key.
I am a monk lock.
   I am a monk key!

The Sugar-Plum Tree

Have you ever heard of the Sugar-Plum Tree?
   'Tis a marvel of great renown!
It blooms on the shore of the Lollipop sea
   In the garden of Shut-Eye Town:
The fruit that it bears is so wondrously sweet
   (As those who have tasted it say)
That good little children have only to eat
   Of that fruit to be happy next day.

My Mother and Your Mother

My mother and your mother
   Went over the way;
Said my mother to your mother,
   It's chop-a-nose day!

Mother Tabbyskins

Sitting at a window
    In her cloak and hat
I saw Mother Tabbyskins,
    The real old cat!
Very old, very old,
    Crumplety and lame;
Teaching kittens how to scold—
    Is it not a shame?

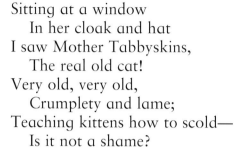

Kittens in the garden
    Looking in her face,
Learning how to spit and swear—
    Oh, what a disgrace!
Very wrong, very wrong,
    Very wrong and bad;
Such a subject for our song,
    Makes us all too sad.

Old Mother Tabbyskins,
    Sticking out her head,
Gave a howl, and then a yowl,
    Hobbled off to bed.

Very sick, very sick,
  Very savage, too;
Pray send for a doctor quick—
  Any one will do!

Doctor Mouse came creeping,
  Creeping to her bed;
Lanced her gums and felt her pulse,
  Whispered she was dead.
Very sly, very sly,
  The real old cat
Open kept her weather eye—
  Mouse! beware of that!

Old Mother Tabbyskins,
  Saying "Serves him right",
Gobbled up the doctor, with
  Infinite delight.
Very fast, very fast,
  Very pleasant, too—
"What a pity it can't last!
  Bring another, do!"

ELIZABETH ANNA HART

Itsy Bitsy Spider

Itsy Bitsy spider
    Climbing up the spout;
Down came the rain
    And washed the spider out.
Out came the sunshine
    And dried up all the rain;
    Itsy Bitsy spider
        Climbing up again.

Little Boy Blue

Little Boy Blue,
    Come blow your horn,
The sheep's in the meadow,
    The cow's in the corn.
Where is the boy
    Who looks after the sheep?
He's under a haycock
    Fast asleep.
        Will you wake him?
        No, not I,
        For if I do,
            He's sure to cry.

Ladybug! Ladybug!

Ladybug! Ladybug! Fly away home,
    Night is approaching, and sunset is come.
The herons are flown to their trees by the Hall;
    Felt, but unseen, the damp dewdrops fall.
This is the close of a still summer day;
    Ladybug! Ladybug! haste! fly away!

EMILY BRONTË

Hickory, Dickory, Dock

Hickory, dickory, dock,
    The mouse ran up the clock.
The clock struck one,
    The mouse ran down,
Hickory, dickory, dock.

Three Blind Mice

Three blind mice, three blind mice!
    See how they run, see how they run!
They all ran after the farmer's wife,
    Who cut off their tails with a carving-knife,
Did ever you see such a thing in your life,
    As three blind mice?

Pop Goes the Weasel

Half a pound of tu'penny rice,
    Half a pound of treacle.
That's the way the money goes,
    POP! goes the weasel.

Little Robin Redbreast

Little Robin Redbreast
    Sat upon a rail:
Niddle-noddle went his head!
    Wiggle-waggle went his tail.

Once I Saw a Little Bird

Once I saw a little bird
    Come hop, hop, hop;
So I cried, "Little bird,
    Will you stop, stop, stop?"
And was going to the window,
    To say, "How do you do?"
But he shook his little tail,
    And far away he flew.

Magpies

One for sorrow, two for joy,
    Three for a girl, four for a boy,
Five for silver, six for gold,
    Seven for a secret never to be told.

Jay-bird

Jay-bird, jay-bird, settin' on a rail,
    Pickin' his teeth with the end of his tail;
Mulberry leaves and calico sleeves—
    All school teachers are hard to please.

Mrs. Hen

Chook, chook, chook, chook, chook,
  Good morning, Mrs. Hen.
How many chickens have you got?
  Madam, I've got ten.

Four of them are yellow,
  And four of them are brown,
And two of them are speckled red,
  The nicest in the town.

I Had a Little Hen

I had a little hen, the prettiest ever seen,
  She washed me the dishes, and kept the house clean;
She went to the mill to fetch me some flour,
  She brought it home in less than an hour;
She baked me my bread, she brewed me my ale,
  She sat by the fire and told many a fine tale.

Tiggy-Touchwood

Tiggy-tiggy-touchwood, my black hen,
  She lays eggs for gentlemen.
Sometimes nine and sometimes ten,
  Tiggy-tiggy-touchwood, my black hen.

Matthew, Mark, Luke, and John

Matthew, Mark, Luke, and John
    Bless the bed that I lie on.
Before I lay me down to sleep,
    I pray the Lord my soul to keep.

Four corners to my bed,
    Four angels there are spread;
Two at the foot, two at the head:
    Four to carry me when I'm dead.

I go by sea, I go by land:
    The Lord made me with His right hand.
Should any danger come to me,
    Sweet Jesus Christ deliver me.

He's the branch and I'm the flower,
    Pray God send me a happy hour;
And should I die before I wake,
    I pray the Lord my soul to take.

How Many Miles to Babylon?

How many miles to Babylon?
    Three score and ten.
Can I get there by candlelight?
    Aye, and back again!

Twinkle, Twinkle, Little Star

Twinkle, twinkle, little star,
    How I wonder what you are!
Up above the moon so high,
    Like a diamond in the sky.

Foxy's Hole

Put your finger in Foxy's hole.
Foxy's not at home.
Foxy's out at the back door
A-picking at a bone.

Star Light, Star Bright

Star light, star bright,
First star I see tonight,
I wish I may, I wish I might,
Have the wish I wish tonight.

I See the Moon

I see the moon,
And the moon sees me;
God bless the moon,
And God bless me.

Here's a Ball for Baby

Here's a ball for baby,
  Big and fat and round.

Here is baby's hammer,
  See how it can pound.

Here are baby's soldiers,
  Standing in a row.

Here is baby's music,
  Clapping, clapping so.

Here is baby's trumpet,
  Tootle-tootle-oo!

Here's the way the baby
  Plays at peek-a-boo.

Here's a big umbrella,
  To keep the baby dry.

Here is baby's cradle,
  Rock-a-baby-bye.

In Dreams

Beyond, beyond the mountain line,
  The gray-stone and the boulder,
Beyond the growth of dark green pine,
  That crowns its western shoulder,
There lies that fairy land of mine,
  Unseen of a beholder.
Ah me! they say if I could stand
  Upon those mountain ledges,
I should but see on either hand
  Plain fields and dusty hedges:
And yet I know my fairy land
  Lies somewhere o'er their hedges.

Baby, Baby Bunting

Baby, baby bunting,
  Father's gone a-hunting,
To fetch a little rabbit-skin
  To wrap his baby bunting in.

The Baby in the Cradle

The baby in the cradle
    Goes rock-a-rock-a-rock.
The clock on the dresser
    Goes tick-a-tick-a-tock.

The rain on the window
    Goes tap-a-tap-a-tap,
But here comes the sun,
    So we clap-a-clap-a-clap!

Go to Bed, Tom

Go to bed, Tom,
    Go to bed, Tom,
Tired or not, Tom,
    Go to bed, Tom.

Lady Moon

Lady Moon, Lady Moon,
Where are you roving?
    Over the sea.
Lady Moon, Lady Moon,
Whom are you loving?
    All that love me.
Are you not tired with
Rolling, and never
    Resting to sleep?
Why look so pale,
And so sad, as for ever
    Wishing to weep?

Dance, Little Baby

Dance, little baby, dance up high,
    Never mind, baby, mother is by;
Crow and caper, caper and crow;
    There, little baby, there you go;

Up to the ceiling, down to the ground,
    Backwards and forwards, round and round;
Dance, little baby, and mother will sing,
    With the merry coral, ding, ding, ding!

Ride a Cock-Horse

Ride a cock-horse to
    Banbury Cross,
To see a fine lady ride on
    a white horse,
Rings on her fingers and
    bells on her toes,
She shall have music
    wherever she goes.

Hush-a-bye, Baby

Hush-a-bye, baby, on the tree top,
    When the wind blows the cradle will rock;
When the bough breaks the cradle will fall,
    Down will come baby, cradle and all.

Rock-a-bye, Baby

Rock-a-bye, baby, thy cradle is green;
    Father's a nobleman, Mother's a queen,
And Betty's a lady, and wears a gold ring,
    And Johnny's a drummer,
        and drums for the King.

Tumbling

In jumping and tumbling
    We spend the whole day,
Till night by arriving
    Has finished our play.

What then? One and all,
    There's no more to be said,
As we tumbled all day,
    So we tumble to bed.

How Many Days Has My Baby to Play?

How many days has my baby to play?
    Saturday, Sunday, Monday;
Tuesday, Wednesday, Thursday, Friday,
    Saturday, Sunday, Monday.

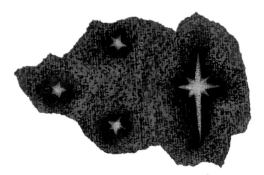

A Cradle Song

Golden slumbers kiss your eyes,
    Smiles awake you when you rise.
Sleep, pretty wantons, do not cry,
    And I will sing a lullaby:
Rock them, rock them, lullaby.

Care is heavy, therefore sleep you;
    You are care, and care must keep you.
Sleep, pretty wantons, do not cry,
    And I will sing a lullaby:
Rock them,
rock them,
lullaby.

The Song of the Stars

We are the stars which sing,
    We sing with our light.
We are the birds of fire
    We fly over the sky,
Our light is a voice.
We make a road for spirits,
    For the spirits to pass over.
Among us are three hunters
    Who chase a bear;
There never was a time
    When they were not hunting.
We look down on
        the mountains.
This is the song of the stars.

Sweet and Low

Sweet and low, sweet and low,
    Wind of the western sea,
Low, low, breathe and blow,
    Wind of the western sea!
Over the rolling waters go,
    Come from the dying moon,
        and blow,
Blow him again to me;
    While my little one, while my
        pretty one, sleeps.

Sleep and rest, sleep and rest,
    Father will come to thee soon;
Rest, rest, on mother's breast,
    Father will come to thee soon;
Father will come to his babe in
        the nest,
        Silver sails all out of the west
            Under the silver
                moon:
            Sleep, my little one,
                sleep, my
                    pretty one,
                        sleep.

Hush, Little Baby

Hush, little baby, don't say a word,
    Papa's going to buy you a
        mocking bird.
If the mocking bird won't sing,
    Papa's going to buy you a
        diamond ring.
If the diamond ring turn to brass,
    Papa's going to buy you a
        looking-glass.
If the looking-glass gets broke,
    Papa's going to buy you a
        billy-goat.
If that billy-goat runs away,
    Papa's going to buy you another
        today.

Hush-a-bye, Don't You Cry

Hush-a-bye, don't you cry,
    Go to sleepy little baby.
When you wake you shall have
    All the pretty little horses.
Blacks and bays, dapples and
        grays,
    Coach and six white horses.
Hush a bye, don't you cry,
    Go to sleepy little baby.
When you wake you shall have
        cake
And all the pretty little horses.

In the Tree-top

"Rock-a-by, baby, up in the tree-top!"
    Mother his blanket is spinning;
And a light little rustle that never will stop,
    Breezes and boughs are beginning.
Rock-a-by, baby, swinging so high!
Rock-a-by!

"When the wind blows, then the cradle
    will rock."
    Hush! now it stirs in the bushes;
Now with a whisper, a flutter of talk,
    Baby and hammock it pushes.
Rock-a-by, baby! shut, pretty eye!
Rock-a-by!

Bed in Summer

In winter I get up at night
    And dress by yellow candle-light.
In summer, quite the other way,
    I have to go to bed by day.

I have to go to bed and see
    The birds still hopping on the tree,
Or hear the grown-up people's feet
    Still going past me in the street.

And does it not seem hard to you,
    When all the sky is clear and blue,
And I should like so much to play,
    To have to go to bed by day?

The Sun Descending in the West

The sun descending in the west,
   The evening star does shine;
The birds are silent in their nest,
   And I must seek for mine.
The moon, like a flower,
   In heaven's high bower,
With silent delight
   Sits and smiles on the night.

Farewell, green fields and happy groves,
   Where flocks have took delight;
Where lambs have nibbled, silent moves
   The feet of angels bright;
Unseen they pour blessing,
   And joy without ceasing,
On each bud and blossom,
   And each sleeping bosom.

The Man in the Moon

The man in the moon,
   Came tumbling down,
And asked his way to Norwich.
He went by the south,
   And burnt his mouth
With supping cold pease-porridge.

The Moon

The moon has a face like the clock in the hall;
    She shines on thieves on the garden wall,
On streets and fields and harbor quays,
    And birdies asleep in the forks of the trees.

The squalling cat and the squeaking mouse,
    The howling dog by the door of the house,
The bat that lies in bed at noon,
    All love to be out by the light of the moon.

But all of the things that belong to the day
    Cuddle to sleep to be out of her way;
And flowers and children close their eyes
    Till up in the morning the sun shall arise.

A Baby Sermon

The lightning and thunder
    They go and they come;
But the stars and the stillness
    Are always at home.

Evening

The day is past, the sun is set,
  And the white stars are in the sky;
While the long grass with dew is wet,
  And through the air the bats now fly.

The lambs have now lain down to sleep,
  The birds have long since sought their nests;
The air is still, and dark, and deep
  On the hill side the old wood rests.

Yet of the dark I have no fear,
  But feel as safe as when 'tis light;
For I know God is with me there,
  And He will guard me through the night.

Here We Are All

Here we are all, by day; by night we are hurled
  By dreams, each one into a several world.

God Be in My Head

God be in my head
　And in my Understanding.
God be in my eyes
　And in my Looking.
God be in my mouth
　And in my Speaking.
God be in my heart
　And in my Thinking.
God be at mine end
　And at my Departing.

Round About There

Round about there,
　Sat a little hare,
A cat came and chased him,
　Right up there!

Hush-a-bye, Baby

Hush-a-bye, baby, they're
　gone to milk,
Lady and milkmaid
　all in silk,
Lady goes softly, maid
　goes slow,
Round again, round
　again, round they go.

My Shadow

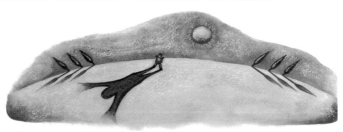

I have a little shadow that goes in and out with me,
    And what can be the use of him is more than I can see.
He is very, very like me from the heels up to the head;
    And I see him jump before me, when I jump into my bed.

The funniest thing about him is the way he likes to grow—
    Not at all like proper children, which is always very slow;
For he sometimes shoots up taller like an india rubber ball,
    And he sometimes gets so little that there's none of him at all.

He hasn't got a notion of how children ought to play,
    And can only make a fool of me in every sort of way.
He stays so close beside me, he's a coward you can see;
    I'd think shame to stick to nursie as that shadow sticks to me!

One morning, very early, before the sun was up,
    I rose and found the shining dew on every buttercup;
But my lazy little shadow, like an arrant sleepyhead,
    Had stayed at home behind me and was fast asleep in bed.

ROBERT LOUIS STEVENSON

Spellbound

The night is darkening round me,
  The wild winds coldly blow;
But a tyrant spell has bound me
  And I cannot, cannot go.

The giant trees are bending
  Their bare boughs weighed with snow.
And the storm is fast descending,
  And yet I cannot go.

Clouds beyond clouds above me,
  Wastes beyond wastes below;
But nothing drear can move me;
  I will not, cannot go.

Night Sounds

Midnight's bell goes ting, ting, ting, ting, ting,
    Then dogs do howl, and not a bird does sing
But the nightingale, and she cries twit, twit, twit;
    Owls then on every bough do sit;
Ravens croak on chimneys' tops;
    The cricket in the chamber hops;
        The nibbling mouse is not asleep,
          But he goes peep, peep, peep, peep, peep;
        And the cats cry mew, mew, mew,
          And still the cats cry mew, mew, mew.

Good Night

Good night, God bless you,
    Go to bed and undress you.

Good night, sweet repose,
    Half the bed and all the clothes.

Wee Willie Winkie

Wee Willie Winkie runs through the town,
    Up-stairs and down-stairs in his nightgown,
Peeping through the keyhole, crying through the lock,
    "Are the children in their beds, it's past eight o'clock?"

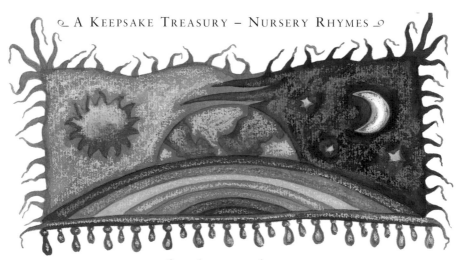

Song of the Sky Loom

O our Mother the Earth, O our Father the Sky,
　Your children are we, and with tired backs
We bring you the gifts that you love.
　Then weave for us a garment of brightness;
May the warp be the white light of morning,
　May the weft be the red light of evening,
May the fringes be the falling rain,
　May the border be the standing rainbow.
Thus weave for us a garment of brightness,
　That we may walk fittingly where birds sing,
That we may walk fittingly where grass is green,
　O our Mother the Earth, O our Father the sky.

A Child's Evening Prayer

'Ere on my bed my limbs I lay,
    God grant me grace my prayers to say:
O God, preserve my mother dear
    In strength and health for many a year;
And, O! preserve my father too,
    And may I pay him reverence due;
And may I my best thoughts employ
    To be my parents' hope and joy;
And O! preserve my brothers both
    From evil doings and from sloth,
And may we always love each other
    Our friends, our father, and our mother.

Come to the Window

Come to the window,
    My baby, with me,
And look at the stars
    That shine on the sea!
There are two little stars
    That play bo-peep
With two little fish
    Far down in the deep;
And two little frogs
    Cry "Neap, neap, neap";
I see a dear baby
    That should be asleep.

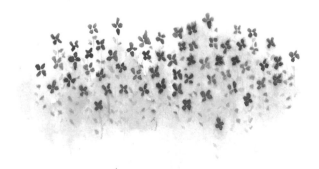

Come to Bed, Says Sleepy-head

Come let's to bed,
  Says Sleepy-head;
"Tarry a while," says Slow;
  "Put on the pot,"
Says Greedy-gut,
  "Let's sup before we go."

O Lady Moon

O Lady Moon, your horns point toward the east:
  Shine, be increased.
O Lady Moon, your horns point toward the west:
  Wane, be at rest.

Lie a-bed

Lie a-bed,
  Sleepy head,
Shut up eyes, bo-peep;
  Till day-break
Never wake:—
  Baby, sleep.

Putting the World to Bed

The little snow people are hurrying down
　　From their home in the clouds overhead;
They are working as hard as ever they can,
　　Putting the world to bed.

Every tree in a soft fleecy nightgown they clothe;
　　Each part has its night-cap of white.
And o'er the cold ground a thick cover they spread
　　Before they say good-night.

And so they come eagerly sliding down,
　　With a swift and silent tread,
Always as busy as busy can be,
　　Putting the world to bed.

Now the Day is Over

Now the day is over,
  Night is drawing nigh,
Shadows of the evening
  Steal across the sky.

Now the darkness gathers,
  Stars begin to peep,
Birds and beasts and flowers
  Soon will be asleep.

Jesu, give the weary
  Calm and sweet repose;
With thy tenderest blessing
  May our eyelids close.

Grant to little children
  Visions bright of thee;
Guard the sailors tossing
  On the deep blue sea.

When the morning waken
  Then may I arise
Pure and fresh and sinless
  In thy holy eyes.

Small is the Wren

Small is the wren,
  Black is the rook,
Great is the sinner
  That steals this book.